stone style

Decorative Ideas and Projects for the Home

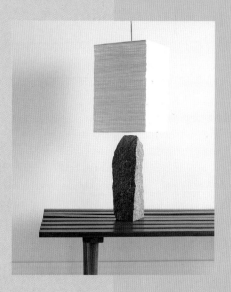

LINDA LEE PURVIS

STOREY
BOOKS

*The mission of Storey Communications
is to serve our customers by publishing practical information
that encourages personal independence in harmony with the environment.*

Edited by Deborah Balmuth and Marie Salter
Art direction and cover design by Meredith Maker
Text design by Susi Oberhelmen
Text layout and production by Susan Bernier
Cover and interior photographs © Margaret Mulligan, except for those marked otherwise and those
   on pages 89, 100, 101 by PhotoDisc; 97 by Michael S. Yamashita/Corbis; and on pages vi, 24,
   33, 44, 56, 63, 68, 69, 77, 86, 92, 106, 108, 109, 111, 116, 136, 138, 139, 140, 145, 148, 151
   by Giles Prett/SCI
Photo styling for Margaret Mulligan's photography by Sharon Dunne
Locations: Cornerbrook Lodge, Zephyr, Ontario; High Fields Country Inn & Spa, Zephyr, Ontario
Illustrations by Terry Dovaston and Associates; watercolor illustration on page 69 by Catherine
   Tredway, from her book *Dream Cottages* (Storey Books, 2001)
Indexed by Susan Olason / Indexes & Knowledge Maps

   The information in this book is true and complete to the best of our knowledge. All recommen-
dations are made without guarantee on the part of the author or Storey Books. The author and pub-
lisher disclaim any liability in connection with the use of this information. For additional
information please contact Storey Books, 210 MASS MoCA Way, North Adams, MA 01247.

   Storey books are available for special premium and promotional uses and for customized editions.
For further information, please call Storey's Custom Publishing Department at 1-800-793-9396.

Printed in Hong Kong by C & C Offset Printing Co., Ltd.
10 9 8 7 6 5 4 3 2 1

Library of Congress Cataloging-in-Publication Data

Purvis, Linda Lee.
   Stone style: decorative ideas and projects for the home / by Linda Lee Purvis.
      p. cm.
   ISBN 1-58017-375-6 (alk. paper)
   1. Rock craft. 2. Handicraft. 3. Stone in interior decoration.

TT293 .P87 2001
745.58'4—dc21
                                                                                    2001020516

To Barry my rock, and
to Emylee my pebble.
Both are my cornerstones.

contents

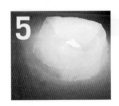

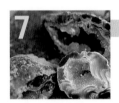

PREFACE

I'M DRAWN TO STONE. I love its simplicity, I'm moved by its energy, and I'm astounded by its variety. Stone is ubiquitous. Virtually anywhere we go, there is a stone within a stone's throw.

My affinity for stone began as a child. I kept lucky pebbles in my pockets and searched tirelessly for the perfect playing piece for hopscotch. I was awed by majestic mountains and enthralled by the wealth of stones at the ocean's edge. And then, as now, I collected them.

From sandstone to shale, granite to quartz, stones are timeless, uniquely appealing, reassuringly weighty and dense. They bear witness to myriad geological wonders, harboring records of early civilizations and preserving traces of organisms long past. Stones speak to us on a primal level, freely sharing their subtle energies and endlessly appealing textures and colors. They're enigmatic, mysterious, compelling.

When we work with stones, incorporating them into our gardens and living spaces, we celebrate their uniqueness. It is my hope that *Stone Style* will fuel your creative energies, pique your curiosity, and inspire you to invite stones into your home. The book features some of my favorite design ideas and step-by-step projects, most of which require only stones and basic tools and materials to complete. Whether you've always been drawn to stones, as I have, or you're just now discovering their simple wonders, *Stone Style* will help you enjoy stones more than ever before.

Give notice to humble stones. They lay in wait for your discovery — to inspire you.

The outline of the stone is round, having no end and no beginning; like the power of the stone it is endless. The stone is perfect of its kind and is the work of nature, no artificial means being used in shaping it. Outwardly it is not beautiful, but its structure is solid, like a solid house in which one may safely dwell.

Chased by Bears
(1843–1915)

ACKNOWLEDGMENTS

To my family, friends, and associates, who have contributed graciously and unconditionally to this project, I extend my heartfelt gratitude. Special thanks to Bob and Margaret Callcott, Cornerbrook Lodge; Charlene and Gerry Keeling, High Fields Country Inn & Spa; Brenda Tucker, Lisa Charlton, J. Murdoch, Laura Scarborough, and Noelene Byrne.

To my husband, Barry, I cannot even begin to count the number of projects that would never have reached completion without your unrelenting, enthusiastic, and motivated support. Dare I say, was that what you anticipated when you said, "I do"? Thank you, forever.

To my young daughter, Emylee, your fluid imagination, ebullience, and incessant rock hounding are an inspiration. I know I'm not a normal mom, but I think you chose me because of that. For this, I adore you.

To my mother, Pearl, who at the drop of a hat was always there to help in whatever way she could; from wrestling with the goats to minding my girl, you've never let me down. Thanks.

To my sister Deb, who has always believed that we are limited only by what we choose for ourselves. Thank you.

And, finally, to Deborah Balmuth, Editorial Director at Storey Books, I extend my humble appreciation for your good sense, professional approach, and kind nature. Working with you has been an absolute joy.

Innocently we begin, picking up a stone here and a stone there, not understanding why we do so but collecting them nonetheless. As time passes, we may become diehard rock hounds, constantly searching for stones worthy of our growing collections. From these rather modest beginnings, with stones serving as both medium and inspiration, the pebblesmith is born.

pebblesmithing
THE ART OF WORKING WITH STONE

A *pebblesmith* is one who actually does something with that prized stash of stones — one who revels in rocks, bringing passion, imagination, and creativity to the earth's bountiful stony harvest. Whether a pebblesmithing activity yields sophisticated or whimsical effects, each effort is sure to satisfy and inspire.

So how does a budding pebblesmith get started? Reading this book is a fine first step. I invite you to become my apprentice, if you will, discovering how to bring stone into your home in ways that are both functional and endlessly gratifying. Let's begin.

THE QUEST FOR THE RIGHT STONE

PERHAPS ONE OF THE most endearing qualities of stones is that they can be found almost anywhere. Whether you walk the beat of a city street or stir up dust on a country road, rocks, stones, and pebbles are there for you, around you, under foot, and within your grasp.

Can you not recall a time when some magical little pebble captured your attention, standing out from the rest, compelling you to pick it up for closer inspection? A unique color, an intriguing surface, or an unusual shape may have been the catalyst for your deliberate effort to touch and retrieve that particular stone. And once your attention had been diverted downward, did you continue to look for an even more outstanding specimen of this common geology, ultimately seeking the best one you could find? I'll bet you did! It's all part of the experience of collecting. You set out looking for one thing and often stumble upon something substantially different but equally fascinating. Be forewarned: Collecting can be addictive if you're not careful.

Okay. So maybe not everyone is like me. Still, I do know that many people collect stones helplessly, as if driven by an unknown force. They forage for and store stones as if stocking food for the longest winter of their lives. And then there are others among us, also lovers of stones and rocks, who would rather not root around in the earth or wade in shallow shores to hunt up collections of stones. Happily, there are rock-hunting options for us all.

NATURE WALKS

If you anticipate combing the landscape for rocks, first consider the qualities of the stone you want, then look where those stones naturally occur. Once you start exploring an area and learn about the type of rock it offers, you'll gain a sense of geological wonderment, amazed by how it all came to be so long ago. Deposits of rock and stone can contrast greatly in areas that are in relatively close proximity, so be sure to take a broad view while hunting for stones.

Smooth Stones. Found near moving water at beaches, on shorelines, and in riverbeds, smooth stones are scoured by silt and sand as the water works tirelessly against the stones' surface, rounding edges and polishing them to an inviting, even texture.

When smooth stones are wet, their colors and patterns are intense and appealing. Yet when they dry, occasionally these favored stones lose their appeal. To make your dry stones look their best, simply restore their watery luster by rubbing them with vegetable oil or jeweler's polish. Alternatively, submerge them in water, perhaps using them to ground floral arrangements or as weighty counterpoints to floating candles.

Sharp Stones. Sharp rocks with jagged edges are often found in mountainous areas or in rugged outcroppings. Usually comprising hard granites and quartzite compositions, sharp stones feature a broad palette of color and often have a distinct, shimmering quality.

Flat and Brittle Stones. Mudstone, shale, slate, and sandstone are predominantly found in areas that used to be under water and can often be identified by bands of color and textures of various thicknesses running horizontally through a mass of rock. Outcroppings of brittle stone can be seen where pressure under the earth's crust caused tremendous shifts, heaving the subterranean floor upward, occasionally redirecting the characteristic bands upward as well. Shale and sandstone are fairly easy to break away. Because the stones are naturally brittle, it's likely bits have already fallen to the ground, making collection easy.

SHOPPING FOR STONES

For those not interested in venturing out into the great outdoors to find stones, there's good news! You can shop for stones. Depending on your interests, you might run down to the local masonry supply yard or home-building supply store to find some rocks. The options available to you for building your stash of stones are quite diverse. And the expense can range from free to — well, it can really add up if you're serious about rocks.

Masonry Supply Yards. Specializing in stone for landscaping and construction purposes, masonry supply yards retail stone and rock of all shapes, sizes, and colors. Often the best places to get a glimpse of the vast diversity of rock available, these yards are great for pebble pickers who don't know where to find the rocks they're seeking. Similar to a stocked trout pond, masonry yards are places where budding rock hounds typically can't miss.

Stores and Shops. Because stones have become popular decorative items, polished pebbles and round river rocks are now available at some home stores, floral outlets, and craft shops. Fine gravel, in a variety of colors and grades, can be found at pet stores and isn't just for aquariums anymore. Go have a look to see what's available locally. You'll be surprised at just how many local options there are for finding stones.

Riverbeds offer an abundance of smooth stones scoured by silt and sand.

ROCK CLASSIFICATIONS

ROCK TYPES VARY in density, composition, grain, and shape, among other things. But basically, there are three classifications of rock — sedimentary, igneous, and metamorphic — each of which is formed in a distinctly different way. Learning more about these rock types and how they are formed may help you in your pebble-smithing and rock-hunting endeavors.

SEDIMENTARY ROCK

Sediment, such as sand, mud, and small pieces of rock, accumulates to form *strata,* or layers. Over long periods of time, these layers are compressed and hardened under the weight of additional sediment deposits, eventually forming sedimentary rock. Fossils are most commonly excavated from sedimentary rock layers.

Fragments of sedimentary rock can be distributed by moving water, wind, and glaciers. Sandstone derives from compressed and hardened sand, siltstone from silt, and shale from clay. Sedimentary rocks are considered soft because they break apart more easily than other rocks, usually in segments between their layers. Small particles can generally be scraped off with ease, making this stone type a good choice for grinding and drilling.

IGNEOUS ROCK

Igneous rock is formed when molten and partially molten material, called *magma,* cools and solidifies. One of the most common forms of igneous rock is granite. A particularly hard stone, granite is composed of glittering micas, smoky quartz, and varying amounts of feldspar, which can dramatically influence the stone's coloring from pink to green. The sparkling crystals detected in granite result from the molten rock having cooled slowly beneath the ground. Igneous rock is stubborn to work with because of its density, but it has great appeal because of its heterogeneous mottling of color and grain.

METAMORPHIC ROCK

As the name suggests, metamorphic rock, which can begin as sedimentary and igneous rock, has undergone some kind of transformation, usually due to intense heat and pressure within the earth's crust. Magma is forced through fissures in the earth's surface as a result of earthquake activity. Rock that is extruded is coarse and light, such as pumice, while magma that doesn't reach the earth's surface is forced out in sheets between old rock layers, forming hard, grainy rocks such as granite.

All types of rock can metamorphose. Shale under pressure becomes slate. Recrystallized calcite in limestone becomes marble. The colors and textures of these rocks vary greatly.

Top left: *Sedimentary rock.* **Top right:** *Igneous rock.* **Bottom left:** *Igneous rock.* **Bottom right:** *Metamorphic rock.*

An Unexpected Find

While searching for some rocks to use in a project, I stopped at an outcropping of rugged shale, rummaging through fallen pieces and breaking away loose chunks that balanced precariously. Then something in the rock I held caught my eye. It was a fossil! I shuddered. I looked at all of the other rocks around me with a hint of wonderment. What secrets do they hold? Can you imagine, if stones could talk, all that they could tell us?

stonefaces and other oddities

W hen you're out hunting stones, keep a watchful eye. You might be surprised by the undiscovered oddities that await your vigilant gaze. A friend of mine retrieved a chunk of rock that fell away from a larger one after being struck and immediately recognized within it the bust of Homer. Some people even explore rock piers and jetties at the waterfront in search of unusual rocks, cast-off remnants of Mother Earth and modern man. With rock hunting, the hunt is sport and the prize merely the luck of the draw. Good luck!

Left: *This haunting stone face was found staring out from a pile of landscaping rocks.* **Right:** *A surprising find, this bust of Homer was "revealed" when the chunk of stone fell away from a larger rock.*

WORKING WITH STONE

WITH A BASIC UNDERSTANDING of pebblesmithing methods, you can become quite proficient. Don't allow the weight and density of rock to stifle your creativity. Special tools make the job easier and, true, some tools are more sophisticated than others, but all can be mastered with time. As with most things, imagination and experimentation will help you discover special techniques of your own that can be tailored to suit your particular interests. With basic tools, a dose of ingenuity, and perhaps a trip to a rental store, you can accomplish almost anything with stone. If the project you have in mind is particularly large or challenging, draw on the experience and expertise of local tradespeople.

TOOLS

Working with rock and stone offers special rewards. There is something inherently satisfying about the mass and heft of stone, and something mystical about its willingness to change at our urging. You'll need to use special tools for some projects covered in this book, but the list of necessary items is surprisingly short.

Many of the tools you need are available at hardware stores and home-building centers. Others may be found at or ordered through companies that specialize in stone products. The following list highlights the tools you might need and gives a general description of how they can be used in your pebblesmithing endeavors.

- **Hammers or mini-sledges** come in a variety of sizes and weights and are used with chisels and pry bars to break stone; alone they can be used to break slate into shards. Choose a weight that you can handle comfortably, being sure that it's heavy enough to carry out its appointed task.

- **Splitting axes** split large rocks and boulders with ease.

- **Chisels** are used in conjunction with hammers and mini-sledges to split and shape rock. Manual and air-driven varieties are available.

- **Water-cooled drill presses** are used for drilling holes in stone. The running water hook-up constantly flushes water over the bit and stone, keeping them cool.

- **Drill bits** are generally available in sizes from ½ inch (1.3 cm) to 2 inches (5 cm). Diamond-matrix coring bits, which have diamond chips impregnated into the metal base, are most commonly used with hard stone like granite. Softer rock that may more willingly yield a hole can sometimes be drilled with carbide-tipped or silicone-carbide bits. Look for bits used for masonry, tile, and glass.

- **Manual hand drills,** though somewhat antiquated, can "drill" a hole when struck with a hammer. Rotate the hand drill after each strike and repeat the process until the drill breaks through.

- **Pry bars and crow bars,** in conjunction with hammers and sledges, are used to split rock. Insert the blade into a crevice and then pound.

Dress for Safety

Rock shards, chips, and dust can be hazardous to the eyes and lungs. Whenever you cut, drill, or work with stone, take appropriate precautions. *Always* wear:

- **Eye protection**
- **Dust mask (or respirator if substantial amounts of sand or dust are involved)**
- **Waterproof jacket or apron when using water-cooled saws and drills**
- **Ear protection for prolonged exposure to loud equipment**
- **Waterproof gloves when cutting and drilling with water-cooled equipment**

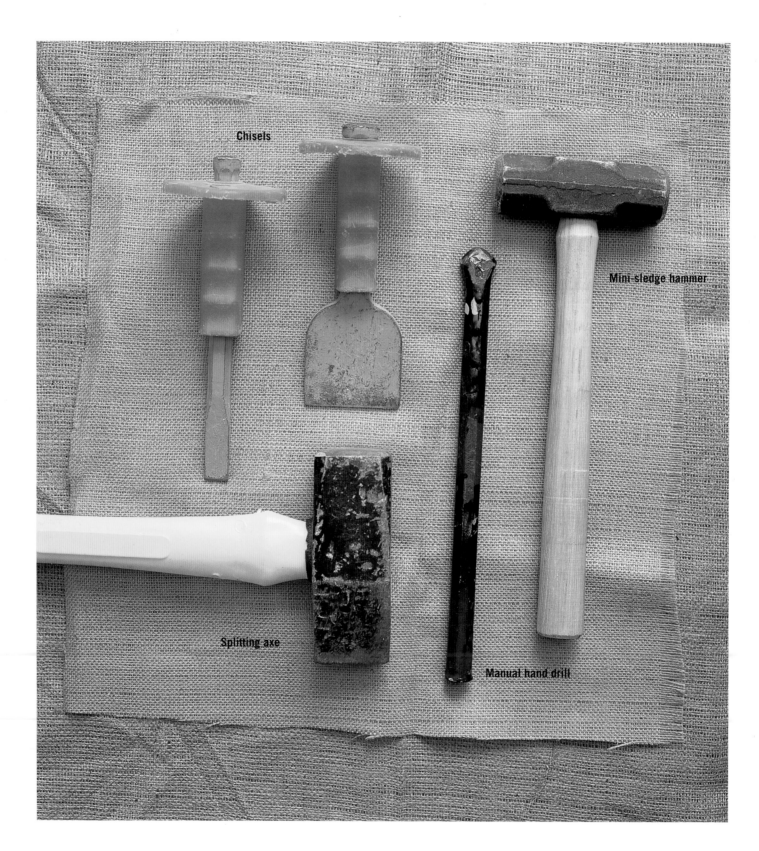

Chisels

Mini-sledge hammer

Splitting axe

Manual hand drill

• **Table saws** outfitted with a diamond-matrix tool blade and a water reservoir keep both the blade and the stone cool while cutting. This setup is ideal for the hobbyist, while more elaborate machines are designed for professionals. Huge table saws with 12-foot (3.6 m) beds are used in manufacturing large stone slabs into stone counter tops and other large items. The blade must always be wet.

• **Tile-cutting saws** are smaller versions of the table saw, again with a water reservoir beneath the table that cools the blade and rock while cutting.

If you're curious about the performance of a saw used for cutting stone, consider renting one and experimenting with it before you buy. You'll learn what the saw can do and what its limitations are — valuable information if you have special tasks or projects in mind. If you have trouble locating diamond bits and blades at your local hardware or home-building supply store, contact a local company that uses them in their trade, explain your situation, and ask if they might be willing to order them for you.

TRADESPEOPLE

When working with stone, you may occasionally need to use specialized industrial tools and equipment or call on tradespeople to help you accomplish your goals. For this reason, especially for large or complex projects, it will be to your advantage to consult with local tradespeople, inquiring whether they might be willing to assist you if the need should arise. In my experience, tradespeople are generally willing to oblige such requests. Sandblasting, rock cutting, and rock drilling are probably what you'll need the most help with as you start out.

Sandblasting. In sandblasting, a stream of sand projected by compressed air is used to etch away fine particles. Tradespeople may undertake this discipline as generalists or as specialists, whose work may range from the automotive industry to brick resurfacing to monument making. Artists with sandblasting equipment also are excellent resources and no doubt will relate to your desire for creativity. Contact local arts associations for leads on such people, or look under MONUMENTS in the Yellow Pages.

Rock Cutting. For large rock, cuts can often be made at masonry-supply or stone yards that sell rock and boulders. Monument companies and manufacturers of marble and granite countertops and fireplaces will be able to assist you in cutting hard stone. Ceramic installers are a good bet for assistance in cutting thin stone like slate or sandstone. And as you might expect, stone masons and bricklayers can also prove quite helpful.

Rock Drilling. Drilling soft stone is fairly easy, but if you need to drill larger holes or holes in hard rock, consult stone countertop manufacturers who drill holes in stone to fit taps and faucets. Some stone yards have drills on site but if not should be able to direct you to local trades that can help.

Locating Other Materials

While stone is the principal constituent of most projects that follow, some do require other materials that are easily found in local craft stores, department stores, lumber yards, and home-building supply stores. Before beginning any project, review the materials and equipment lists to be sure you have all needed supplies on hand.

Left: *Hand tools commonly used when working with rock*

2

Stone isn't reserved just for chimneys and fireplaces anymore. It can work well virtually anywhere in the home, imparting an earthy ruggedness that complements the texture and scale of our living spaces. Versatile and adaptable, stone makes a dynamic statement when used as part of a bold presentation, yet remains modest and playful when cleverly fashioned into home accessories.

tones of stone
HARMONY IN THE HOME

Stones need not dominate your decorating style to be appreciated. They can accent the home environment in simple ways without stirring a fuss. They are merely rocks, after all, having rested quietly in the landscape for centuries, barely noticed, just waiting for the right moment to come inside. With the vast array of stones available, it's easy to integrate stone into your personal decor. You'll see.

barn-board-and-pebble plant stand

PLANTS CAN TRANSFORM A RIGID, angular living space into one that's cozy and inviting, introducing depth, texture, and color. Fancy pots, window boxes, urns, and stylized containers abound in flower shops, nurseries, and garden boutiques, all contributing to eye-catching and trendy pottings of our favorite plants.

The challenge comes when we try to place our plants to best advantage, so they receive the light they need and we can see the planters we've searched so long and hard to find. Achieving the desired balance between form and function isn't always easy, but this window-box planter can help. It's designed to give longer legs to short pots, without totally consuming them as traditional window boxes would. The base of the stand is lined with galvanized sheet metal and filled with pebbles, which offer excellent drainage. With this planter, you can enjoy the beauty of distinctive pots and thriving plants.

Barn board is a friendly companion to stones and clay pots. However, this project can easily be adapted for a less rustic feel by using lumber that is nicely stained and finished. When selecting twigs for the base, choose willow, maple, or alder. Avoid twigs from pines and spruces and other sticky sap trees.

MATERIALS

Barn board planks, 1 x 10
20 Nails, 2" (5 cm), for box
4 Twigs, 1½ to 2" (3.8–5 cm) in diameter, for legs
4 Screws, 2½" (6.3 cm)
4 Twigs, 1" (2.5 cm) in diameter, for supports
24 Nails, 1¼" (3.2 cm), for supports and crosspieces
4 Twigs, ¾" (1.9 cm) in diameter, for crosspieces
Galvanized sheet metal, 30 gauge; available in 16" x 36" sheets (40 cm x 90 cm)
Silicone sealer
Vinegar (optional)
Galvanized metal primer (optional)
Oil-based paint
Pebbles, from pea-sized gravel to grape-sized pebbles

EQUIPMENT

Ruler/measuring tape
Saw
Hammer
Screwdriver
Pruning saw or loppers
Dark marking pen
Gloves (optional)
Tin snips
Hand seamers or wide-edge vice grips
Hammer
Rag (optional)
Paintbrush (optional)

Stand Dimensions

Measure the width and height of the area below a window to customize a plant stand for that particular spot. Alternatively, if you already have pots in mind for the stand, measure their width — at the widest point — when lined in a row or as you plan to position them in the box. To determine leg length, consider the desired height of the pots in relation to the window and the average height of the plant species you wish to grow.

Our box has interior measurements of 24 inches (60 cm) long, 10½ inches (26.3 cm) wide, and 2½ inches (6.3 cm) high. The bottom of the box sits 24 inches (60 cm) above the floor. Instructions for this size stand follow.

TIP: Barn board is often uneven. Always consider and measure board thickness when cutting lumber to size.

project continues on page 14 ▶

The Box

1. Cut the bottom board first. Then cut a board to correspond to the width of the bottom board's shortest side. Rip this board lengthwise with the saw to the desired height, but remember to include in your calculation the thickness of the bottom board. For example, our box interior height is 2½ inches (6.3 cm); we add 1 inch (2.5 cm) to account for the thickness of the bottom board to which the side will be nailed, giving us a total side height of 3½ inches (8.8 cm). Nail the short sides in place as shown below.

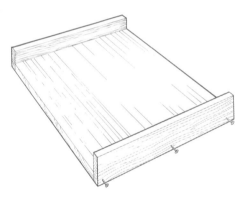

2. To get the measurement for the long edge, measure from the outer edge of one short side to the outer edge of the other. Cut a board to this length, and then rip it lengthwise to the same height as the short sides, 3½ inches (8.8 cm). Nail in place.

Legs and Supports

3. Cut four 24-inch (60 cm) leg pieces from twigs of approximately the same width. Prop the box to hold it steady, or have someone hold it steady for you, while you position the first leg. Then sink a screw through the top, down into the leg. Do the same for all four legs.

TIP: If the barn board is particularly old, it may be helpful to predrill holes before attempting to secure the legs with screws.

4. Cut two 28-inch (70 cm) support twigs for the front and back of the stand. Position them on the legs about 8 to 10 inches (20–25 cm) above the floor, then nail in place.

5. Cut two 14-inch (35 cm) support twigs for the sides of the stand. Position them 8 to 10 inches (20–25 cm) above the floor, then nail in place.

6. Cut four 26-inch (65 cm) crosspieces. Nail two crosspieces to the front and back of the stand, as shown. Alternatively, measure a diagonal line from the top of the leg to the center of the support that spans the stand's length, then add 2 inches (5 cm) to that length. Cut four crosspieces and secure.

TIP: Hold a brick firmly behind the joint when nailing a crosspiece to a support. This prevents the twigs from bouncing while being struck.

7. With a pruning saw or loppers, trim the excess length from the crosspieces. If the legs do not rest evenly, trim excess off the longest leg(s) with a pruning saw.

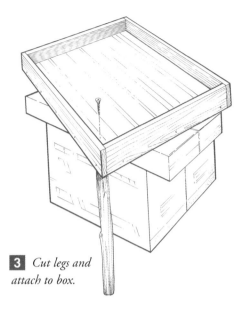

3 *Cut legs and attach to box.*

5 *Cut and attach supports to legs.*

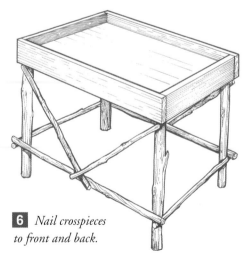

6 *Nail crosspieces to front and back.*

The Liner

8. Using the interior measurements of the box, *less* ½ inch (1.3 cm) on all sides, draw the box bottom on the sheet of metal. Then draw onto the box the four sides, being sure to include the interior height *plus* ½ inch (1.3 cm). Draw a line on the outermost edges, ½ inch (1 cm) from the top, to indicate the safety edge. On each side of the two end pieces draw a tabbed corner.

9. Wearing protective gloves, carefully cut the liner with tin snips, following the lines drawn.

10. With the hand seamers or vice grips, align the edge of the tool to the ½ inch (1.3 cm) safety edge. Grip and bend the entire length of the metal edge toward the inside of the box. Go over it again, this time using the seamers to crimp the fold closed. Repeat on other three edges.

11. When the safety edge is complete, bend upward the four tabs at each end, aligning them so they are perpendicular to the flat box. Then, hammer the four sides up at a 90-degree angle to form the box. The end tabs will automatically line up in their proper position on the outside of the four corners.

12. Slip the liner into the wooden planter box to ensure a tight fit. Seal all gaps in the liner with silicone. Allow to dry overnight. *Note:* If you prefer an unpainted look, go directly to Finishing Touches.

13. Remove liner. With a rag soaked in vinegar, wipe down the liner's interior and all exterior sides (excluding bottom). The vinegar reacts with the sheet metal, etching it so it will accept the primer. Let dry completely.

14. When the liner is dry, paint the liner's interior and all exterior sides (excluding bottom) with metal primer. Let dry.

15. With oil-based paint in a color that complements the wood and pebbles, paint the liner's interior and all exterior sides (excluding bottom).

Help with Sheet Metal

If preparing the metal liner is more than you care to do or if you choose to make numerous plant stands, you might opt to contact a sheet metal fabricator. Check the Yellow Pages for listings under HEATING CONTRACTORS and SHEET METAL. Give the fabricator the required dimensions and a cutting layout (step 8), and the rest will be accomplished easily with specialized equipment.

Finishing Touches

Fit the finished liner into the stand and fill to the top with pebbles. Gently settle the pots into the pebbles so that they are sturdy and straight. Position the planter where you wish, and enjoy!

Give your plants the water they require, but avoid filling the trough excessively, as the water may stagnate. The liner is designed to catch surplus water that flows through the plants, offering excellent drainage and valuable humidity as the water evaporates.

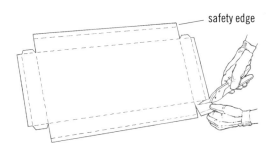

9 *Cut the liner with tin snips, following the lines drawn.*

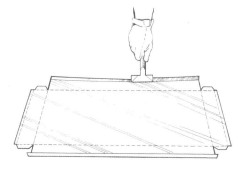

10 *Grip and bend safety edge toward inside of box.*

11 *Hammer four sides up at a 90-degree angle to form box.*

decorative tiles

TILE-DECORATING IS INCREDIBLY SATISFYING. It requires little time, space, money, or equipment, and appeals to crafters of all skill levels. Tiles can become anything you want them to be. Flat or raised, large or small, colorful or neutral, purposeful or playful, they offer something for everyone.

For this project, you'll purchase inexpensive tiles that will serve as the base for your decorative efforts. Tiles are available in a range of sizes, from small bathroom tiles to large floor tiles. Typically, tiles are square, though some tiles are available as diamonds and rectangles. If you've got a particular shape and size in mind for your project, tile cutters can help you customize tiles to suit your needs. Tiles with a matte finish on both sides will work best for this project; unglazed terra cotta tiles are ideal.

Using some grout, pebbles and stones, glass chips and jewels, shells, broken chinaware — virtually anything — you can create clever and diverse mosaic designs for a multitude of places and purposes. And because the tiles are decorated one at a time, you can work on small individual pieces or plan ahead to incorporate several tiles into a larger piece. An afternoon tile-decorating session with the whole family can produce a collection of uniquely beautiful tiles, with results reminiscent of the individual fabric squares made during a quilting bee.

MATERIALS

Tiles, preferably unglazed, sized for your project

Tile grout for kitchen and bath, or mortar patch compound

Glass shards/chips, stones, or other decorative items

Backing material (wood board, tray, etc.)

Paint (optional)

White glue (optional)

EQUIPMENT

Newspaper

Tile cutters (optional)

Pliers (optional)

Putty knife or spreader

Jar

Container of water, wide mouth to fit knife/spreader

Glass nippers or mosaic cutters (optional)

Paintbrush (optional)

Paper towels (optional)

Decorating a Tile

1. Spread newspaper over the work surface. Make sure tiles are free of dirt, grease, and residue. If you are making a custom-sized piece, cut tile(s) to the desired size with the tile cutter. Score the tile, then break it apart by snapping the excess downward. If the remnant is too small to grasp by hand, use pliers.

2. Using the putty knife or spreader, scoop some tile grout or mortar patch from its container. Spread an even ¼- to ½-inch (0.6–1.3 cm) layer over the matte surface of the tile, including the edges. The thickness of the grout layer depends on the depth of the materials you wish to sink into it; glass chips require less grout than stones, for example.

project continues on page 18 ▶

3. With the putty knife, scrape clean the edges of the tile as you work, keeping the grout edge straight and smooth. When grouting is complete, rest the tile on top of a large jar or something similar for easy access.

TIP: Drop the knife/spreader into a container of water to keep compound soft for quick cleanup later.

4. Lightly place the decorative items on the tile's wet surface in a pattern of your choice, leaving a narrow border of grout all around the outer edge. Gently press the items into the grout to secure them well.

TIP: If you want to use glass shards or glass chips to decorate your tile, be sure to prepare them before you grout the tile. Group the different decorative items in plastic containers on your work surface, so everything is organized and accessible to you when you're ready to create your design.

5. Allow the tile to dry for 24 hours.

Mounting Tiles

6. Make sure the backing material (wood board, tray, etc.) you've selected is clean; I like to seal wood surfaces with a coat of paint. Position tiles on the backing as you wish. Apply a spiral of glue to the back of each tile and affix firmly to the backing. Let dry overnight.

7. If tiles are spaced apart or have no border around their outer edges, carefully apply tile grout or mortar patch using a narrow putty knife or your finger. Dip the knife or your finger in a container of water for easier application. Smooth grout or mortar evenly to fill in any gaps.

8. If you wish to add embellishments to the backing, do so *after* the grout or mortar is applied but *before* it sets. Covering freshly applied grout or

Grout or Mortar?

Prepared grout and mortar patch are easy to use, but if you prefer you can buy unprepared packages and make your own. Unprepared mortar is available in colors other than white. Choose whichever binding agent is most appropriate for your particular project.

Mortar patch looks gray and gritty, while wall-tile grout is typically white, silky smooth, and almost shiny. If you'll be using your tile in a high-maintenance area, grout is easier to clean than mortar, but the decorative items you choose to use may make cleaning challenging no matter the binding agent.

Nestle plain tiles and decorative tiles in a bed of pebbles for a dramatic composition.

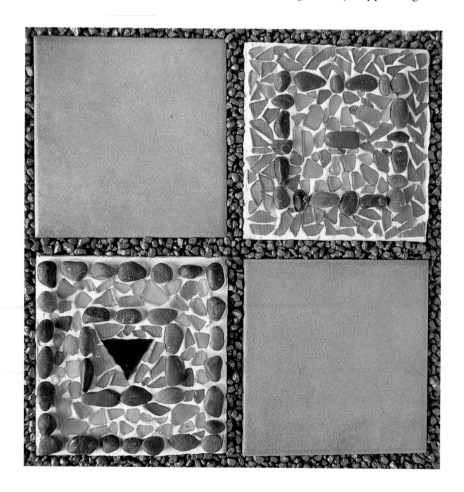

mortar with damp paper towels slows the drying process and gives you more time to work.

9. Use the putty knife to scrape edges clean if the panel will be installed in a wood frame. If the panel will be hung, grout or mortar the raw edges to conceal the backing material.

TIP: If you are making a panel that will be mounted on a wall, leave some spots on the backing free of mortar or grout for easier mounting with screws. Otherwise, attach picture hangers to the backing.

What to Do with Decorative Tiles?

Here are just a few ideas to help you start thinking about how to incorporate decorative tiles into your home. The possibilities are almost endless, so use a little imagination to customize your own collection.

- **Use decorative tiles as a backsplash for a sink area, or as wall accents for a kitchen, bathroom, or partition.**
- **Intersperse them with standard tiles of similar size, or join them together in an eclectic symphony of color and texture.**
- **Frame individual stand-alone decorative tiles as works of art.**

Top: *Designs can be representational, as in this stone garden.* **Bottom:** *Abstract designs can be geometrical or free form.*

stone mosaic bench

MATERIALS

Spruce or pine board, 1 x 12, 4½' long (1.4 m)

10 Screws, 1¼" (3.1 cm)

Paint or stain

Mortar patch compound

Pebbles, glass chips, other embellishments

24 Nails, 1½" or 1¾" (3.8 or 4.4 cm)

EQUIPMENT

Ruler

Pencil

Saw or jigsaw

Sandpaper

Screwdriver

Paintbrush

Putty knife/spreader

Wet paper towels

I LOVE THE ROUGH, GRITTY TEXTURE between the stones on this mosaic-type bench. At first glance, it has a casual garden quality, but it also can be quite elegant depending on how you choose to finish it. Easy construction makes it fast and fun to make. As with the decorative tile project, I'm sure you'll want to make more than one of these.

Select decorative items that complement a particular room's decor or that contrast with it to produce an eclectic effect. Slate pieces, pebbles, glass shards, shells, and similar materials can be juxtaposed to create wonderful patterns in the neutral mortar background. (The mosaic technique for this project is identical to the one used for decorative tiles on page 17). You might arrange multiple benches in small groupings to hold plants, decorative artifacts, or any number of other items. Whether you choose to refurbish an old stool or tabletop with this technique or start from scratch, you're sure to find the end result both functional and pleasing.

Constructing the Bench

1. Cut one 24-inch (60 cm) board for the bench top and two 12-inch (30 cm) pieces for the legs. Sand down any burrs on the leg pieces.

2. Mark each leg piece according to the cutting layout at right. Using a jigsaw, cut a V notch at the base of each leg piece.

3. Attach the legs to the bench, as shown on page 22, driving screws down from the top. Be sure that legs are perpendicular to the bench before securing them.

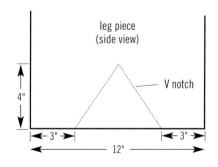

2 *V-notch cutting layout.*

project continues on page 22 ▶

4. Cut a 4-inch (10 cm) square board in half diagonally to form two triangular leg support pieces. Attach these pieces to the bench, as shown at right. To fasten the support for each leg, drive one screw up through the support into the underside of the bench and drive another screw through the support into the leg.

5. Rip the remaining board lengthwise into 3-inch (7.5 cm) strips. Measure the width of the bench and cut two lengths to that size.

TIP: Remember that boards are not the size their names might suggest (a 2 × 4 is actually 1½ × 3½ inches, for example), so always take accurate measurements.

6. Measure the thickness of each side piece, then add that total to the length of the bench. The total will be approximately 26 inches (65 cm). Sand the ends of each board to remove burrs. Set aside.

Decorating the Bench

7. Paint or stain all wood surfaces, including the bench top, to the desired color to seal them.

8. Using the putty knife or spreader, scoop some mortar patch compound from its container. Spread an even ¼- to ½-inch (0.6–1.3 cm) layer over the bench top only. Scrape clean the edges of the bench top as you work, keeping the mortar edge straight and smooth.

9. Decorate the bench top with stones and other items. When the design is complete, loosely drape wet paper towels over the entire surface to slow

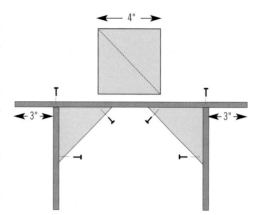

4 *Cut square board in half diagonally and attach supports to bench.*

the drying process and reduce the potential for cracks in the mortar. Let the bench top dry for at least 24 hours.

TIP: Consider how you'll use the bench before selecting decorative items. Smooth, flat glass pieces and pebbles will yield an even surface; larger, more prominent decorative items may limit how you can use the finished bench.

Securing the Sides

10. With the putty knife, scrape off any dried mortar from the sides of the bench top.

11. Attach the short sides to the bench top, being sure that the tops of the sides are flush with the decorated mortar. Nail through each side piece, securing it to the bench top.

12. Attach the long side pieces to the bench top, ensuring that the boards are flush with the decorated mortar and the ends of the short sides. Nail through each side into the bench top.

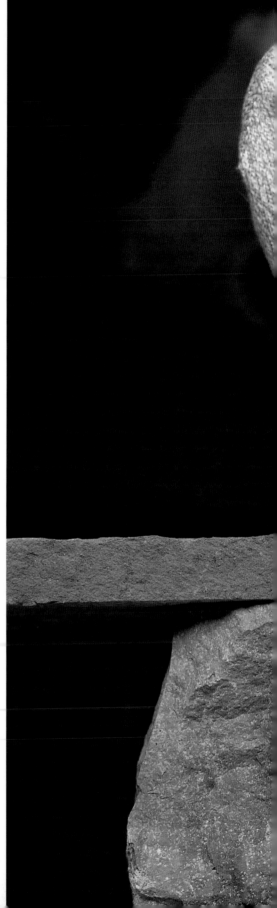

A simple, sturdy stone bench can be made by resting a slab of flat stone atop two blocks of evenly cut stone.

stone slab shelves and tabletops

Wandering around a stone yard is a dangerous activity when you're extremely partial to stone. Indeed, it seems that every piece of stone I spy either suggests a purpose for itself or has such a unique character that I know it will be perfect for something, eventually.

Many of the stone pieces at a yard are precut, even if only on one side. These make ideal shelves. To hang a stone shelf, simply mount brackets onto a wall (being sure to anchor screws securely in the joists) and set the stone slab across the top of them. Because the stone is heavy, it's not likely to budge on its own. Stone shelves with an uneven surface offer a sense of abandon, making them excellent for displaying things randomly, perhaps at slightly different heights.

Stone slabs that make interesting tabletops range from smooth slate to uneven flagstone. Choose the stone that best suits the intended purpose of the table. For example, if you'll just be setting coffee cups on the table, then almost any surface will do. Harvest legs for your stone table from urn stands, old tables, ottomans, or wrought-iron stands, or make legs from heavy chunks of stone, which can often be found precut in the stone yard. Rest the stone slab on the legs you've chosen to determine the stability of the table; generally, wide spread support is best.

If you've selected stone legs for your table and merely balancing the slab on the stone legs does not offer reliable support, apply a special stone and concrete adhesive (available at home-building supply stores) to secure the tabletop to the legs. It goes without saying that permanently joining a stone tabletop to stone legs makes for a heavy table, so consider its placement carefully. You'll need several strong hands to move it elsewhere.

Above: *Stone slab shelves can be mounted almost anywhere; be sure brackets are well secured before decorating the shelf with special keepsakes.* **Right:** *If you have a penchant for rustic furniture, a flagstone and twig side table will be a welcome addition to your home.*

pebble mirror

THE POSSIBILITIES ARE ALMOST ENDLESS with this simple mosaic technique. It can be applied to any number of unexpected treasures-in-waiting, found at garage sales, inventory clearance sales, or in your own attic. Mirror frames and old picture frames with nothing left to brag about can be brought back in style with minimal fuss. Banging together a simple frame from scrap wood allows you to customize this project to suit your needs.

By experimenting with different patterns, colors, and embellishments, you can easily transform a plain frame into one that's highly textured, muted with earth tones, or flamboyantly bedazzled with color. Choose decorative items that appeal to you. Pebbles, glass shards, smooth jewels, rhinestones, beads — almost anything — will rest comfortably in the bed of gritty mortar that awaits. And the results are sure to please.

MATERIALS

- Wooden picture or mirror frame
- Picture hanger, sawtooth or eye-hook (optional)
- Wire for picture hanging (optional)
- Acrylic paint, gray
- Mortar patch compound
- Pebbles, glass chips, decorative embellishments of your choice

EQUIPMENT

- Masking tape (optional)
- Rags
- Small paintbrush
- Putty knife or spreader
- Container of water

1. If the frame has a mirror in it, cover the mirror with strips of masking tape. If there's no hanger on the back of the frame, add one appropriate for the weight of the finished project.

2. With a dry rag, rub the surface of the wooden frame to remove any dust and dirt. If the inside or outside edge of the mirror frame won't be mortared, paint it and let it dry completely. Then with a clean wet rag, rub the surface of the frame to dampen it.

3. Using the putty knife, scoop a generous amount of mortar patch onto the frame. Spread a smooth, even ¼ inch (0.6 cm) layer over the front and sides of the frame. If you wish to embed large items into the mortar, a slightly deeper layer will be required. Smooth to an even finish. Place putty knife in the container of water to keep mortar soft for easy cleanup.

4. Lightly place the decorative items on the wet mortar randomly or in a pattern of your choice. When you are satisfied with the pattern, gently press the items into the mortar. Push the items into the mortar just far enough to secure them well. Allow the frame to dry for 24 hours.

5. With the putty knife, remove any rough burrs of mortar that may have clung to the frame's edges. Remove the masking tape from the mirror.

Creating a Mirror from a Frame

If the frame you've selected lacks the backing needed to secure mirrored glass, cut a piece of cardboard to the exact dimensions of the glass, and place the cardboard behind the glass in the frame opening. Tap small finishing nails partway into the frame, parallel to the glass; the exposed nail ends will secure the glass and cardboard backing in place. Alternatively, take the frame to a frame shop where you can have the backing fastened by a professional.

memory box display

Most of us collect objects as mementos of our experiences — places we've been, people we've met, things we've done. From photographs to pamphlets, key chains to postcards, we all treasure items that conjure fond memories of a special time or place.

When I travel, my favorite collectible is usually a little piece of rock — nothing necessarily beautiful or extraordinary, just one that sits inconspicuously in the landscape, perhaps even under foot. And when friends are traveling to distant places and offer to bring me a souvenir, I usually ask for a stone that they've discovered on their journey — and its story. I want to now where it came from, how it was found, and what they were doing the day they selected it for me; all of this creates a visual memory.

Stones are easy to carry and cost just a moment to pick up. As long as they are clean and don't have soil on them, transporting stones from one country to another is usually not an issue. If you are in doubt, check with your national Customs Service.

One of the challenges of collecting stones is how best to keep and display them. Photos and stamps can be easily cataloged in books. Ball caps and key chains can be kept on hooks. Pamphlets and postcards can be stored away flat. But rocks? In numbers, they're heavy; in shape, they're obscure; and to mount, they're awkward. What's a rock hound to do? A memory box display will neatly house your prized pebbles.

A curio cabinet or knickknack shelving is ideal for housing a collection of small rocks. You might inscribe each stone with its location of origin and the date it was found, or you can keep a separate legend to which you can refer for identification. Assign one rock or a small related grouping to each compartment, and voilà!

For a more varied memory box display, consider adding other found objects: feathers, shells, twigs, and the like complement each other well and add character to your cobbled junket fare. Each time you view your collection, you'll be granted moments to reflect on the adventures that led to your finding these natural treasures.

Left: *Sheet moss provides a comfortable bed for the special items displayed in this memory box.* **Right:** *Almost anything that holds interest or meaning for you is worthy of display, like this pocketful of treasures from a beach outing.*

sandstone wall clock

IT REALLY DOESN'T MATTER WHAT A CLOCK LOOKS like as long as it keeps good time. It's true — a clock can be made from almost anything. A broken piece of slate or sandstone can provide the perfect counterpoint to the sweeping hands of time. Though this clock's surface is left pleasingly plain, its irregular shape can add visual interest to any room. Choose a piece of sandstone or slate appropriate for the size of clock you wish to make, paying careful attention to the stone's thickness. Clock hubs come in a number of sizes, 1 inch (2.5 cm) or less being the most common. Larger hubs are available from specialty clock shops.

MATERIALS

Sandstone or slate

Clock workings

Numbers 1–12 in a style of your choice (optional)

Pebbles, twigs, or buttons (optional)

EQUIPMENT

Chalk

Ruler/tape measure (optional)

Drill with ⅜" (1 cm) bit to accommodate clock hub

Quick-setting epoxy

1. With chalk, mark where on the stone the clock hub will be placed. If the stone has a recognizable geometric shape, it's usually best to center the hub.

TIP: To find the center of the stone, lightly draw two lines, from corner to corner, on the front of the stone. The point where the lines intersect is the center.

2. Drill an appropriately sized hole for the clock hub from front to back. When a drill bit breaks through stone, it's not uncommon for a small shard of chunk of stone to break away. By drilling from front to back, any accidental breakage will be reserved to the back of the clock, hidden from view.

TIP: Most standard-sized clock hubs require a ⅜-inch (1 cm) hole, however, do not assume this is the case. Read the manufacturer's installation instructions before drilling the hole.

3. Insert the clock hub, which is attached to the clock workings, battery compartment, and hanger assembly, from back to front. Follow manufacturer's instructions for the appropriate order in which washer, hands, screw, and finial should be attached to the hub on the front of the clock. Assembly is easy and can be completed by hand.

4. Check to see how the clock will hang, and adjust if necessary.

5. If you wish to indicate hours on the clock face, use numbers, pebbles, twigs, or buttons, and attach them with epoxy. Be sure that hands can sweep freely past any additions.

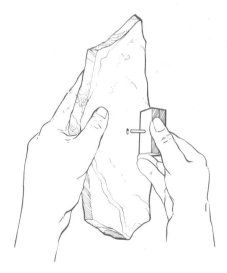

3 *Insert clock hub from back to front.*

bookends and other rock rests

Wander through any stone yard and you'll see a grand assortment of precut stones that already have straight edges — perfect for bookends. Some of these rocks require only a coating of vegetable oil or jeweler's polish to accentuate their grain and give them a finished look. Whether used singly or in pairs, rock bookends offer weight, versatility, convenience, character, and style.

Other rocks have a naturally flat side, making them perfect for painting. Use acrylic paint to decorate the rock as you wish. Seal the painted rock with latex varnish to protect it for year's to come. Decorated rocks make lovely doorstops. Or use a rock au naturel for the same purpose.

Keep a selection of clean rocks on hand to act as page holders for open books. Use rocks as paperweights to keep notepapers and newspaper clippings from scattering about.

Clean rocks make ideal page holders for open books.

A simple rock paperweight will keep things in order when summer winds whisper.

WHILE STUDYING ARCHITECTURE in Valparaíso, Chile, Gabriel Cortez became a disciple of María Martner, a well-known Chilean sculptor who used stone in her powerful murals. Gabriel fell in love with María's stonework and soon mastered her art.

In 1986, Gabriel relocated to Toronto, Canada, and, after working for five years in an unrelated field, was encouraged to seek an artistic career, pursuing his passion for stone. Cortez and his wife-to-be, Roma, mounted an impressive exhibit at a prominent show in Toronto, where their work was met with great approval. One of their first large commissions was a mosaic medallion made of natural stone, 14 feet in diameter, for the dining area of

NATURAL-STONE MOSAICS

GABRIEL CORTEZ

the Mövenpick Marché Restaurant in Toronto. In 1995, Gabriel and Roma embarked on a new joint venture: ArtStone by Gabriel Cortez.

Gabriel develops designs and molds for three-dimensional pieces — birdbaths, garden benches, fountains, and tables, among them — to which he then applies his natural-stone mosaic technique. Each piece of natural stone is chosen specifically for its color and shape and is then embedded in concrete reinforced with galvanized wire mesh and polymer-based bonding agents, which combat fluctuations in temperature and changing environments. ArtStone pieces work equally well indoors and out.

Left: *Art Stone medallion at Mövenpick Marché Restaurant, Toronto.* **Top right:** *Round birdbath.*
Bottom right: *Detail of flower mosaic. (Photos by Gabriel Cortez)*

3

During a great famine, a stranger visited a village where food was scarce. The villagers initially discouraged his stay, only to learn that he wished to make a pot of delicious stone soup for all to share.

The stranger produced an ordinary stone from a worn leather pouch and dropped it into a pot of boiling water. He tasted the broth with satisfaction, exclaiming how much he loved stone soup but noting that stone soup with cabbage was

stone soup

ENTERTAINING WITH STONE

even better. Caught up in the stranger's generous spirit, a villager dropped some cabbage into the pot. Delighted, the stranger said that a hint of salt beef would make the soup even better. A bit of salt beef was added to the pot, and so it went. Soon onions, carrots, and potatoes were added until the soup became a fine meal.

Moral: When we work together, each contributing what we can, the results are wondrously good. And the good can begin with something as simple as a stone.

SETTING A TABLE WITH STONE

WITH AN INTERESTING assortment of rocks, a supply of fresh flowers, and a good meal, stones make perfect dinner companions. The ideas featured in this chapter are bound to invite friendly conversation throughout a quiet evening and possibly for days to come. Rocks and stones can be used to ground floral arrangements. Slate slabs make unique serving platters and trays for easy-to-serve foods, like hors d'oeuvres, cheeses, and fruit. And frosty pebbles do a yeoman's job of keeping even the finest of wines perfectly chilled.

Stones of all shapes and sizes easily find a home in the dining room, and because you can customize your stone display to suit the scale of your table, stones make willing collaborators. The visual appeal and integrity of stone allows you to simplify flower arrangements, particularly when preparing them for large table settings. The diverse pigmentation of stones complements any color scheme and imparts a hint of whimsy fitting for even a formal dinner party.

In addition to beautiful floral displays that set the stage for delightful dinnertime drama, many supporting roles in the overall production can be played by stones. With an open, creative mind, consider the stones you have on hand and imagine what roles will use them to best advantage. For example, flat slabs of rock and rocks with flat surfaces work well as serving platters and as trivets, and are excellent bases for pillar and votive candles. When decorated, small palm-sized stones make unique place markers for dinner guests. Make choices suitable for your table requirements and dinner menu. Use interesting, unexpected combinations of stone as the foundation for your next repast.

Left: *Use sturdy stone slabs as fabulous alternative serving plates for grapes, cheese and crackers, hors d'oeuvres, cookies, and candies. Wash serving stones in soap and water, rinse, wipe with a mild bleach solution, rinse thoroughly, and let dry.*

Put small stones in a freezer overnight to get them frosty cold. Place the frigid stones in a pot or ice bucket, alone or with ice chips, to keep bottles of wine perfectly chilled. Chilled stones mixed with ice retain their cold temperature longer than ice alone.

Above: *Spare floral arrangements in simple rock vases are wonderfully organic and visually dramatic.*

Left: *Small rocks of various shapes and sizes make attractive chopstick rests. Beautifully made sushi looks striking when presented on a slab of stone; sandstone and slate are excellent choices.*

loose-pebble trivet

THE OPERATIVE WORD FOR THIS PROJECT IS *LOOSE*. This casual trivet makes an ideal nesting spot for odd-shaped containers, piping hot teapots, and steaming serving bowls. The pebbles' earth tones provide a pleasing visual contrast to a multitude of vessels and, if you wish, you can paint the trivet's wooden frame to match a particular color scheme. You can easily achieve a refined or rustic look by choosing your pebbles accordingly; smoothly polished river stones provide a touch of elegance, whereas coarsely finished granite shards have a rugged appeal.

Whatever your taste, this trivet will accommodate with ease hot pots and bowls of all types. Unlike fabric trivets that serve mainly to protect the surface underneath, this trivet traps heat and actually helps to keep your dishes warmer longer.

MATERIALS

**Spruce or pine board, 1"
(2.5 cm) thick**

1½" (3.8 cm) finishing nails

Wood stain or acrylic paint

**Wood sealer (with optional
color)**

**Pebbles, from pea gravel to
¾" (1.9 cm)**

EQUIPMENT

Table saw

Measuring tape/ruler

Pencil

Sandpaper, medium grit

Hammer

Punch (optional)

Paintbrush, 2" (5 cm) tip

1. Select a 1-inch-thick (2.5 cm) spruce or pine board (any grade) in an 8-, 10-, or 12-inch width (20, 25, and 30 cm, respectively). Cut the board to a length of 8, 10, or 12 inches. This is the trivet base. (The board's width determines the size of the square trivet.)

TIP: Remember that boards are not the size their names suggest (a 2 x 4 is actually 1½ x 3½ inches, for example), so always take accurate measurements.

2. Make the side pieces. Use a table saw to rip a board lengthwise to a width of approximately 2½ to 3 inches (6.3–7.5 cm).

3. Take a precise measurement of one side of the trivet base. Cut two side pieces to this length. Sand side pieces to remove burrs. Nail sides flush to opposite ends of trivet base. Countersink nails with a punch.

4. Measure the width of the base with sides in place (for example, width of trivet base plus 2 inches (5 cm) if a 1-inch-thick (2.5 cm) board is used for sides.) Cut the final two sides to that length. Sand the side pieces to remove burrs. Nail sides flush with base, as shown at right. Countersink nails with a punch.

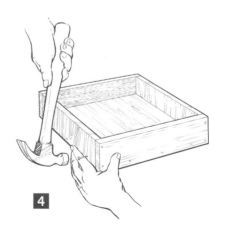

4

project continues on page 44 ▶

5. Use a wood stain or acrylic paint (thinned with water) to cover the trivet base. One or two coats, with sufficient drying time between each, should suffice. Finish with one or two coats of a varnish, Varathane by Flecto (Oakland, California), or wood sealer, following the manufacturer's directions. This will keep your trivet base waterproof, making it easy to clean with a damp cloth.

TIP: Save some time by using a wood-sealing product that applies color as it seals, such as Polyshades by Minwax (Upper Saddle River, New Jersey).

6. Add pebbles of your choice. Fill the trivet base no more than ½ inch (1.3 cm) from the top, which allows pebbles to shift when items are placed on the trivet.

TIP: Clean soiled pebbles in a colander under running water to keep the trivet looking its best. No machine washing is necessary!

hot rocks

Rock is so dense that it retains heat extremely well. Bring warmth to your table by heating a slab or a few nuggets of stone in a warm oven for several minutes. Wrap the stones in a cloth napkin or tea towel and place in the bottom of a bread basket to keep breads and rolls delightfully warm while serving. Use a flat stone as a warming trivet under teapots and casseroles.

A large slab of stone can be set on the bottom rack of a cold oven, then warmed when the oven is preheated. Place breads and baked goods directly on the stone for even heating and golden results.

Left: *Heat a flat rock in the oven at about 250°F (121°C) or 10 to 15 minutes. Wrap it carefully in a cloth napkin or tea towel, then place it in a bread basket beneath heated bread or rolls to keep them warm throughout the meal.* **Above:** *Use flat rocks as warming trivets to protect table surfaces. Affix felt or a bit of cork to the underside of rocks used for this purpose to avoid accidentally scratching the surfaces you wish to protect.*

bucolic centerpiece

BECAUSE BOTH COME FROM NATURE, flowers and rocks make excellent decorating companions. Bring these outdoor elements into your home any time of year for a delightful pick-me-up. Dismal, gray days that sink us into the doldrums are easily remedied with these special gifts from nature. The sights and smells of fresh foliage and flowers, combined with the sensual, stable presence of stone, can enliven any room or table setting.

Arrangements of flowers and rocks should be simple and unaffected, in keeping with nature. With the aid of a few florist supplies, such as kenzans and water tubes, you can simulate natural-looking assemblages of rocks and flowers, as individual displays or in combination, such as the large table-length arrangement featured here. It's all quite simple to do, and though the show is big the cost is little. You'll amaze yourself and your guests with the results.

MATERIALS

Kenzans (pinholders for flowers)

Small waterproof containers to accommodate kenzans

Flat rocks (optional)

Selection of rocks proportionate to table size

Selection of fresh flowers and foliage

Other accessories (optional); see Other Ideas on page 48

EQUIPMENT

Sharp knife

1. Place each kenzan in its own water-proof container, then cover with about an inch (2.5 cm) of water. Custard cups and plastic food containers of the right size work well, as they will be hidden beneath the flower arrangement.

2. Distribute the containers randomly down the center of the table on which you wish to set your display, leaving sufficient space between them.

TIP: To protect the table's finish, put felt beneath the rocks and plastic beneath the water containers or set water containers directly on flat rocks.

3. Begin placing rocks in an irregular line down the center of the table or along the back of the table if the display is for a one-sided buffet. Lean or stack additional rocks against and on top of those placed previously. Use the rocks to conceal the water containers, leaving the kenzans accessible from the top.

4. Cut flower and foliage stems as you work, then insert them securely into the kenzans, working on the whole display simultaneously. Start by establishing the height of the display, then work from the bottom up. The largest, darkest, or most fully opened flowers are

Flower Selection and Care

- **Cut or purchase fresh flowers one day in advance for your display.**

- **Choose flowers that are similar in size or that graduate in size from large to small.**

- **Select stems with flowers that are just starting to open and that have plenty of tight buds, to ensure optimal freshness and blooms. Include some unopened buds in your designs.**

- **Place floral preservative in luke-warm water. This nourishes the flowers and inhibits growth of harmful bacteria, which can cause early fading.**

- **Recut flower stems with a sharp knife before putting them in the preservative solution.**

project continues on page 48 ▶

considered the focal point for the display and so should be positioned closest to the base. Relative flower size generally should diminish from bottom to top. Insert stems vertically as much as possible. When arranging clusters of blooms, remember that they should be somewhat sparse so as not to appear out of balance with the small-diameter base. Stagger heights from kenzan to kenzan to add a sense of spontaneity.

5. Add foliage to further conceal base. Place any remaining small rocks or other decorative accents on and around the mound of flowers and rocks.

6. Add fresh water to the kenzan containers daily if the display will remain in place for a period of time.

Other Ideas

• Put single stem flowers in plastic water tubes, and position the tubes between rock crevices. This adds visual interest low to the table.

• Garnish rocks and the table with fresh flower petals.

• Incorporate driftwood, shells, vines, feathers, or other items specific to your theme.

• Make the most of negative space. *Negative space,* or the space around your display, allows you to highlight individual flowers or small groupings. An open design also allows you to do more with fewer materials, all the while giving a sense of completeness.

• Place the flowers in a thin row down the center of the table, highlighting the somewhat sparse outcrop-

pings by staggering heights and clustering sizes. Unify the arrangement with an uninterrupted bed of rocks at the base. For a buffet table set against a wall, position the display at the back of the table, providing a stunning backdrop for the food before it.

• Create arrangements for every season. Incorporate evergreen boughs and holly in winter, crocus and other flowering bulbs in spring, and autumn leaves in fall.

• Tailor the display for specialty parties, from birthdays to weddings, by incorporating party themes using the same basic design techniques.

• If setting the display in an outdoor setting or if your table's surface is sufficiently durable, mist water from a plant sprayer on the display to darken the stones' colors and give the fresh appearance of dewdrops on the blooms.

buds at top

fully opened
flowers at base

loose leaves

water tube

kenzan (base of each cluster)

Right: *Make a frosty pebble centerpiece by placing riverbed pebbles in the bottom of a ring mold, filling it with water, then freezing. Invert the frozen mold onto a deep dish, surround it with moss and twigs, and illuminate with tea lights for an otherworldly effect.*

table-decorating ideas

Dress up stones with pretty handmade papers, and wrap them with shiny wire or sparkling cording. Then write the guest's name on a small card and tie it to the rock as you would name tag to a package. If you have access to a tile saw, another economical option would be to lightly score a rock with the saw blade. The rock is thus transformed into a reuseable base for a decorative place card.

Use smooth stones to direct guests to their place settings. Paint your guests' names on the stones or have the names sandblasted for a more sophisticated look. For an outdoor wedding reception, paint a rock with the name of each guest, noting the appropriate table number on the underside. The rocks double as memorable tokens of the day and offer a personal touch that can't be bought. They are especially suited to outdoor receptions that brisk breezes might otherwise plague.

When using tablecloths for outdoor gatherings, uninvited winds can become a nuisance, but wired-and-ribboned rocks can help. Twist wire around a few medium-sized stones, and then fasten the stones to contrasting- or complementary-colored ribbons or fabric strips that will be draped across the table in several places to weigh down the cloth. Wired rocks can also be attached to small clips that are randomly fastened to the edge of the cloth. Match the look of these rocks to the rocks used on your tabletop for an artful presentation.

stylized stone

S tone can be fashioned to suit any number of purposes. Stone bowls are rugged, functional art pieces. The shallow bowl *(opposite)* was sandblasted from black granite by Mark Richardson (see profile on page 102).

Stone coasters are easily made from cut pieces of slate or marble tile. Simply affix felt backing to each coaster, then enjoy worry-free refreshment whenever you wish.

Left: *A rugged stone bowl displays kumquats in a dramatic still life of color and texture.*
Above: *Slate and tile pieces make excellent coasters. They are simple, natural, stackable, and appropriate for mugs of any size. Affix felt or a bit of cork to the underside of each coaster.*

This Zen dining room features a table that is six-feet square and can seat up to twelve people. Made of French Limestone, the table has two textures. The center is textured with ridges, and the twelve-inch border is honed, producing an interesting, sensual contrast. Though it may look sleek and peaceful, the table weighs nearly 1,000 pounds and required five men to install. The floor is made of limestone, in the fashion of Stone Parquet.

JEAN-JACQUES FERRON, TOGETHER WITH HIS WIFE, Carole Boy Ferron, run Modern Stone Age, a gallery showroom of stone crafts and architectural elements in New York City. Since its inception fifteen years ago, Jean-Jacques continues to combine environment, stone, and lifestyle, designing stone architectural elements for interior applications. With the renewed interest in objects of the earth, the store has found a niche.

Jean-Jacques worked with plastics for a time but was concerned by the environmental impact of the medium and didn't feel that it was totally aligned with his creative vision. Stone, on the other hand, was ideal, having

CONCEPTUAL STONE ART
JEAN-JACQUES FERRON

timeless appeal, earthly beauty, and natural abundance. When Jean-Jacques left plastics for stone, he surmised that we had come full circle, to what was a new, modern Stone Age.

Jean-Jacques strives to reach new heights with stone, designing objects that are functional as well as beautiful. From sinks to dinnerware, he designs stone pieces for every room of the home.

Modern Stone Age designs spaces and interiors. This simple, understated spa powder room features a curved wall covered with small, honed marble mosaic. The sink is carved from a block of Carrera marble. (Photo by Philippe Houzé, Black Diamond, New York)

4

Stone complements any home interior. As functional as it is beautiful, stone can be used any way you wish — in large, decorative stand-alone pieces that can become focal points for a room, or in small, understated utilitarian pieces like the ones featured in this chapter. The possibilities are almost endless.

stone details

ACCENTING THE HOME WITH STONE

If you're not sure how to begin using decorative stone accents, study the ideas that follow. Group like objects in small collections that invite visual exploration. Use stones in decorative, functional, and innovative ways for delightfully pleasing results.

rock 'n' wire photo holder

THIS EASY-TO-MAKE PHOTO HOLDER is a creative alternative to framing and an ideal way to mount large numbers of photos without a lot of expense or fuss. Display photographs individually or in small congregations of varying heights. A thoughtful gift for the photographers in your life, this photo holder is an ideal way to display images that are frequently changed and updated. The same holder can be used to hold place cards for your next dinner party, art identification tags, special messages, and special-occasion greetings.

MATERIALS

Soft rock (soapstone, sandstone, lava rock, soft marble) with one flat side

Stovepipe wire or strong, malleable wire, approximately 18 gauge

Superglue or quick-setting epoxy

EQUIPMENT

Safety glasses

Drill and masonry or carbide bit, smallest on hand

Needle-nose pliers

Wire cutters

1. Rest the rock, flat side down, on the work surface.

2. Wearing safety glasses, center the drill bit over the rock and drill a small vertical hole, at least ¼ to ½ inch (0.6–1.3 cm) deep, into the top.

3. Cut a 10-inch (25 cm) length of wire. With needle-nose pliers, shape as desired. Begin at the center of your design, carefully bending and spiraling the wire, all the while trying to keep the spaces between the wire roughly equal. Repeat the shape at least twice to secure photos.

4. When you are satisfied with the shape of the wire, bend the trailing end of the wire *away* from the design, at a 90-degree angle, to form the stem. With wire cutters, trim the stem to the desired length, taking into account the depth of the predrilled hole.

5. Place a drop of superglue or epoxy into the predrilled hole. Insert wire stem and hold securely until the glue sets. Let dry as directed before use.

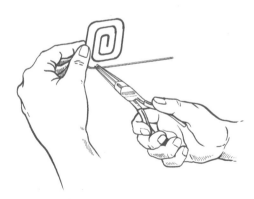

3 *Shape wire with needle-nose pliers.*

5 *Insert wire stem in predrilled hole.*

stone knobs

SIMPLICITY IS A CORNERSTONE OF STYLE. So if you want to add a dash of panache that won't overwhelm understated decor, try these decorative stone knobs. They bring a contemporary, rustic charm to the kitchen, bedroom, and anywhere else neglected knobs need a new look. These knobs look great and work well on drawers and cupboards that receive average use. Stones, twigs, and hardware should be proportionate in size to the furniture on which they'll be used. The sizes given in the Materials list are for standard-sized knob replacements.

MATERIALS

Stones of equal size, approximately 1¼" (3.1 cm); polished if preferred

Young twigs, no more than half the diameter of the stone

Quick-setting epoxy

Washers, ³⁄₁₆" (5 mm)

No. 8 screws, ¾" (1.9 cm)

EQUIPMENT

Pruning shears

Clamp

Slip-joint pliers

Drill and wood bit, ⅛" (3 mm)

Screwdriver (optional)

1. If you wish to change knobs and pulls that you already have, you can probably reuse the existing hardware. If not, measure all dimensions carefully (thickness of drawer, size of drilled hole, etc.) and choose sizes of hardware and stone accordingly.

2. With pruning shears, cut ½-inch (1.3 cm) twig pieces.

3. Clamp a twig piece to the end of the workbench. Drill a ¼-inch (0.6 cm) pilot hole through the center of the twig. Repeat for each twig piece.

4. Set the drawer or cabinet door face-up, if possible.

5. Put a washer on a screw, then insert from the *back* of the drawer face or cabinet door, through the predrilled hole. *Note:* If a drawer or cabinet door has no predrilled hole, drill one.

6. Grasp a predrilled twig firmly with your fingers, placing screw tip into hole, then tighten the screw firmly with a screwdriver.

TIP: Overtightening the screw can split the twig, so use gentle pressure until the screw is secure.

7. With epoxy, attach a stone to the end of the twig. Be sure that twig end and stone are glued flush. Let set until dry.

TIP: If drawer face or cabinet door is positioned vertically, hold knob firmly in place until glue sets to prevent slippage.

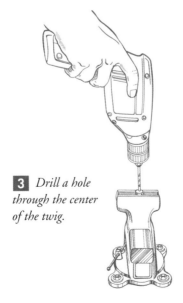

3 *Drill a hole through the center of the twig.*

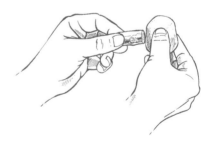

7 *Attach a stone to the end of the twig.*

slate trinket box

EVERYONE CAN USE A TRINKET BOX, and because you'll make this one yourself it can be any size you'd like. Customize the box to hold a specific item, or consider it an opportunity to use up any odd pieces of slate that you might have. There are two ways to make this unpretentious box — the first is easy and the second is even easier. In Method 1, stone is cut to size, allowing you to make the box as large or as small as you'd like. In Method 2, five like-sized marble tiles are used to make the box and no cutting is required.

Method 1

1. Use a ruler and felt-tip pen to draw on the slate a cutting plan for the sides of the box. Each side measures 3½ inches (8.8 cm) by 4½ inches (11.3 cm). Wearing safety glasses, cut sides to size with the tile-cutting saw.

2. Attach the sides to each other with epoxy to form a box. Let set until dry.

3. Place the box on top of a piece of raw slate. With a felt-tip pen, trace the box's *interior* dimensions onto the slate. Because the width of each box side may differ, this step allows you to custom-fit the base to the box. Wearing safety glasses, cut the base to size with the tile-cutting saw.

4. Apply epoxy to each edge of the base, then slip the box securely over it, being sure to position the box precisely as it was traced. Let set until dry.

TIP: If the box is positioned incorrectly, the box will not fit snugly over the base.

5. Top with a lid. Choose either precut tumbled marble tile or, if the size is appropriate, an irregular uncut piece of slate or other flat stone.

6. With epoxy, affix a stone knob to the center of the lid. If you'd like to add feet, attach a stone to each corner of the box base with epoxy. Let set until dry.

TIP: This same method can be used to make a stunning slate candle box. Lay out and cut the pieces for the slate box. Embellish one or more sides by drilling a pattern of holes; snowflakes, stars, and geometric shapes all work well. Assemble the box. Place a tea light in the box, light, and enjoy. Caution: Never leave a lit candle unattended.

Method 2

1. Select five marble tiles.

2. Apply epoxy to the four outer edges of the base tile. Attach a side piece to each edge. Let set until dry.

3. Cut bits of twig or bamboo to the height of the box. Affix them to the empty channels on each corner of the box to help stabilize it.

4. Choose a slightly larger tile or an irregular, natural flat stone for a lid. With epoxy, affix a stone knob to the center of the lid. If you'd like to add feet, attach a stone to each corner of the box base with epoxy. Stones should be approximately the same size. Let set until dry.

stone magnets and tacks

H ow many magnets and tacks do you have? Even though I've got lots, I can always use more. Add to your collection by making some decorative magnets and tacks of your very own. With quick-setting epoxy, simply affix flat, lightweight stones to the heads of magnets and wood tacks. Allow them to dry for 24 hours, then use them with gusto. Stone-topped magnets and tacks can liven up even the busiest refrigerator-art galleries and bulletin boards.

Stone magnets and tacks also make thoughtful, inexpensive gifts. A small decorative box fitted with foam holds stone tacks upright for pain-free removal. Arrange magnets in a small, shallow tin for a neat display.

A collection of stone magnets safeguards a collage of treasures.

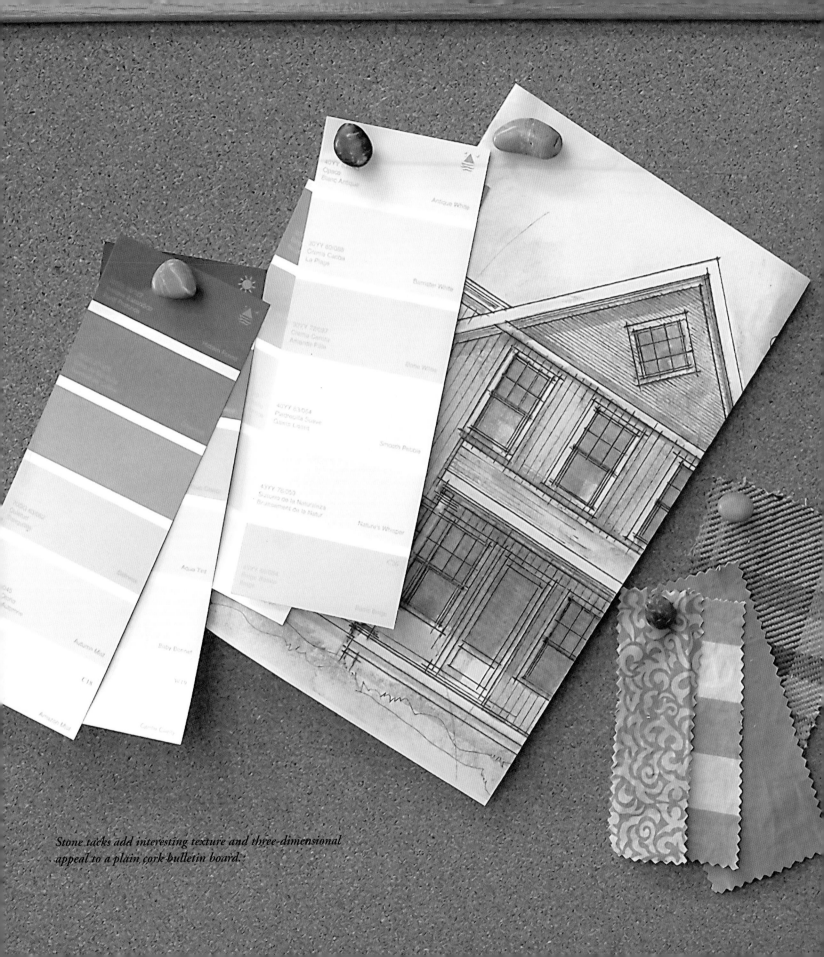

Stone tacks add interesting texture and three-dimensional appeal to a plain cork bulletin board.

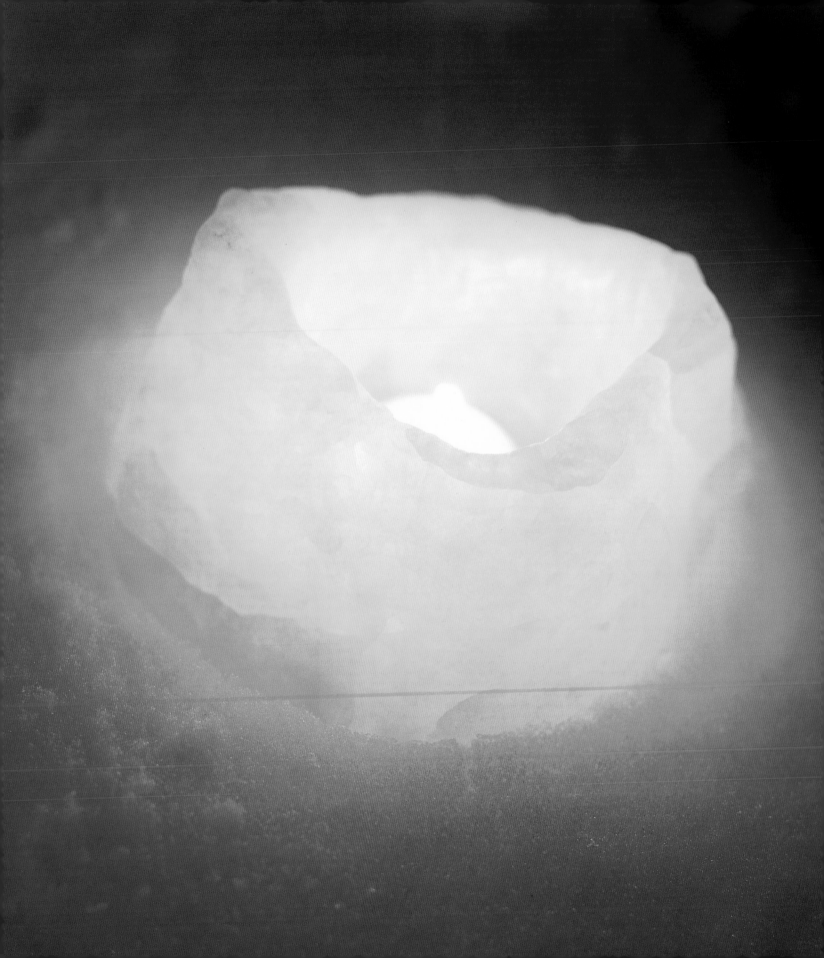

5

Candles and soft incandescent lighting cast a warm, almost magical glow on the body of stone. With its natural heft and stability, stone is a logical accompaniment for all types of lighting fixtures. The texture and quality of light can dramatically alter the mood of any room. Use new light sources with weighty stone bases to brighten your home as twilight falls.

illuminated stone
ROCK-INSPIRED CANDLES AND LAMPS

If you want to make a traditional table lamp, search for stones that have a naturally occurring flat side. If a stacked-stone lamp base is more to your liking, seek out slate, shale, and other soft, flat stones. Candleholders can be made easily from virtually any stone type.

CANDLES AND STONE

THOUGH WE RELY on it daily, artificial light simply cannot compare to the magical, energetic light cast by a single flame. Candles offer lighting that is dramatic, unique, and ever-changing. When used in combination with the varied, irregular textures of stone, candles provide unmatched ambience.

Slabs of flat stone serve well as foundations for groupings of sturdy pillar candles and small votives, while protecting table surfaces. Holes can be drilled into larger, fuller rocks to hold narrow tapers. Naturally fire resistant, stone is a perfect partner for candles. Cluster candles of varying heights and sizes in front of a darkened window or mirror to double their dramatic effect when lit. *Caution:* Never leave a burning candle unattended.

Candles cast a mystical light, especially in the evening. Here, candles of varying shapes and sizes are set out on raw stone slabs and in fitted stone candleholders for a stunning display. In the event that you have a stone candleholder with a hole of nonstandard size, simply roll a candle to fit from a sheet of beeswax.

stone lantern

NOTHING QUITE COMPARES with a flame's flickering dance. This quaint stone lantern houses a charming, subtle light that cavorts merrily behind the bamboo lattice. The stone walls give it a primitive, Old World feel, while the bamboo suggests the charms of the Far East. Perfectly suited to a garden room or entranceway, the lantern looks stunning both indoors and out.

MATERIALS

Flat stone pieces

Small round stone

Quick-setting epoxy

Bamboo, large and small canes

Tea light

EQUIPMENT

Ruler/tape measure

Tile-cutting saw (optional)

Newspapers

Felt-tip pen

Adhesive tape

Saw

Pruning shears (optional)

Disposable paintbrush

Cotton swabs

Green sheet moss (optional)

Selecting and Preparing Stones

1. Choose four flat pieces of stone of similar size and shape for the top, bottom, and sides of the lantern. Slight irregularities in the stone add character to the lantern but must not interfere with how the pieces fit together, as this will compromise the stability of the finished piece.

2. If you're unable to find like-sized stones, cut stones down to size with the tile-cutting saw. You'll need two side pieces, approximately 5 inches (12.5 cm) by 5½ inches (13.8 cm), and a piece for the base and for the roof, each approximately 10 to 12 inches (25–30 cm) square.

3. Fit the pieces together to get a sense of how they will look when the lantern is assembled.

Securing the Sides

4. Cover your work surface with newspaper. Place the lantern's base, flat side down, on the work surface, with what you envision to be the front edge of the stone facing you.

5. Center the lantern sides on the stone, spanning them about 5 to 6 inches (12.5–15 cm) apart, or placing them where they rest best. With a pen, mark on the base the placement of each side's *interior* edge. An extra pair of hands is extremely helpful for this step.

6. With a paintbrush, apply a generous amount of epoxy to the bottom edges of the side pieces and position where marked. Prop with a box or books, and secure with adhesive tape. Let dry for several hours before continuing assembly.

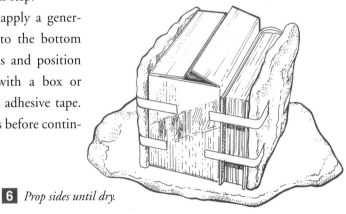

6 *Prop sides until dry.*

project continues on page 76 ▶

Assembling the Bamboo Lattice

7. Measure and cut four 5-inch (12.5 cm) pieces of the large bamboo, and six 5-inch (12.5 cm) pieces of the small bamboo for the vertical pieces. Cut small bamboo with pruning shears if you wish. You may need to customize the height of the vertical pieces to accommodate the depth of the roof.

8. Cut six 5½-inch (13.8 cm) lengths of small bamboo for the horizontal lattice pieces. For a custom fit, measure the distance between the interior edges of the sides, then add ⅛ to ¼ inch (3–6 mm) to that total. *Note:* The small bamboo pieces must be long enough to make contact with the stone sides, but short enough that they do not obstruct the large vertical bamboo pieces.

9. Three horizontal pieces are used on each side of the lantern. Do your best to space them equally. With a cotton swab, apply epoxy to both ends of a horizontal piece and hold in place on the lantern side until epoxy sets. Repeat this process for each horizontal piece.

10. Apply epoxy to each large vertical bamboo piece, securing one large piece to each corner.

11. Three small vertical pieces are used on each side of the lantern. Do your best to space them equally. Apply epoxy to each small vertical bamboo piece, and affix to horizontal bamboo pieces, as shown.

9 *Apply epoxy to the bamboo pieces with a cotton swab.*

11 *Affix small vertical pieces to horizontal pieces.*

Finishing Touches

12. Position the roof piece on top of the lantern. Top with a round stone that will serve as a knob. Epoxy the stone knob in place.

13. Place lantern on top of one or more flat rocks to add texture and height.

14. Tuck bits of green sheet moss randomly into crevices, if desired. Lift lid and insert tea light.

floating candles

F loating candles have become quite popular in recent years and for good reason. They're soothing, peaceful additions to the home.

Choose an open glass bowl or container of any size and shape you wish. Line the bowl with river pebbles, add water and floating candles, and voilà — a dramatic centerpiece. Float fresh blossoms of complementary or contrasting colors in the bowl for a lovely, illuminated floral display. Such an arrangement makes a beautiful spring or special-occasion centerpiece.

Tip: Use long safety matches to light floating candles. Light floating candles only *after* they have been placed in water. Never leave a burning candle unattended.

boulder lamp

ROCK HAS AN ENDURING, RUGGED APPEAL, particularly in settings that feature wood and other natural materials. And what better way to integrate rock into your everyday home decor than as a lamp base? Stone's durable, dense composition provides natural stability. This lamp will withstand the test of time. For hard rock, use a water-cooled drill press and a diamond-matrix coring bit. *Note:* If you find a perfect rock that lacks a flat side, buttress the base by affixing another stone to it with epoxy or have it cut to your specifications.

MATERIALS

- **Soft rock with flat base (e.g., soapstone)**
- **Bottle-lamp kit (available at hardware stores)**
- **Lightbulb**
- **Lampshade**
- **Felt or cork furniture protector tabs**

EQUIPMENT

- **Safety glasses**
- **Drill**
- **Diamond-matrix coring bit, ½–1" (1.3–2.5 cm)**
- **Hacksaw**
- **Silicone**

Drilling the Hole

1. Drill into the top of the rock about 1 inch (2.5 cm); be sure to wear safety glasses. The hole must be sufficiently deep to house the base of the light socket and need not go all the way through the lamp base. The diameter of the hole can vary somewhat, from ½ to 1 inch (1.3–2.5 cm), depending on how the light socket is positioned. If the hole is larger than the lamp fitting, the hole can easily be filled in with silicone at assembly. (See About the Bottle-Lamp Kit on page 80.)

2. If you lack the appropriate equipment or are unable to drill into stone, have the hole drilled to your specifications by a tradesperson. (See page 9.) Alternatively, consider purchasing a predrilled rock vase or candle holder, which, if sufficiently large, will work equally well.

Assembling the Lamp

3. Position the light socket in the lamp base to ensure a level fit. Remove light socket.

4. Apply silicone around the hole's inside rim, insert the light socket — again, ensuring a level fit — and secure the socket in place.

5. Insert a bulb of appropriate wattage, and top the lamp with a shade. For smaller lamps, consider using a self-supporting shade (the kind with the wire wings that attach to the sides of the lightbulb), as these tend to be available in smaller sizes. *Caution:* Lightbulb wattage must be appropriate for the lamp hardware and shade. Never exceed the wattage the manufacturer recommends.

6. Apply furniture protector tabs to the bottom of the lamp base.

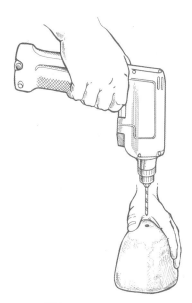

1 *Drill into the top of the rock about 1 inch (2.5 cm).*

About the Bottle-Lamp Kit

As its name suggests, a bottle-lamp kit contains everything you need to make a lamp from a glass bottle or Mason jar, which is then filled with interesting textural materials, ranging from corn kernels to potpourri. The kit includes either a cork top or a Mason jar lid; you provide the bottle or jar. The kit also contains a socket, threaded rod, and electrical wiring needed to create a functioning lamp.

The electrical cord in the kit exits the socket from the side, not from the bottom, so when you insert the socket in the lamp base, the cord will run out behind the piece, not down through it. The socket can rest in the hole on either the narrow threaded rod or the wider, tapering base. Apply silicone around the hole's inside rim before inserting the socket.

Note: If the drilled hole is wider than the tapered socket base, the base will not fit in the hole securely when placed. In such a case, thread the socket onto the rod. Cut the rod to the appropriate depth with a hacksaw, and insert socket assembly into hole. Add silicone to the hole to fill the gap around the threaded rod, then hold the socket assembly upright until the silicone sets.

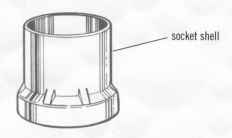

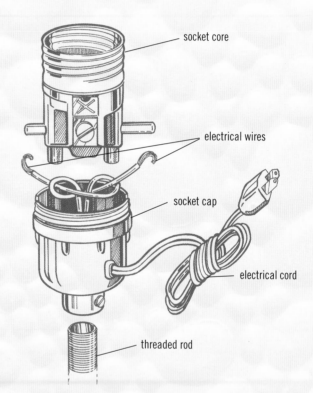

socket shell

socket core

electrical wires

socket cap

electrical cord

threaded rod

KATHERINE AHERN'S LOVE OF NATURE AND AFFINITY FOR LIGHT inspire her signature lamp designs. She chooses natural materials because they contribute to her goal of capturing the essence of soft, late-day light as it filters through trees onto the elements of nature below. Her early stick lamps were inspired by a bunch of leaning birch branches, and the stone lamp is a natural progression: sticks lean; stones stack.

Through her work, Katherine has learned a valuable lesson in not wasting. She rarely collects a stone that she doesn't use, and the weight of the stone dissuades her from wasting her strength.

Katherine spends hours living with and looking at her gathered materials, while contemplating the possible creations that await her liberating touch. Handmade shades crown Katherine's signature lamp designs.

Birch and Willow Studio is located in Boston, Massachusetts. Katherine's work is available at craft galleries and craft shows throughout the United States.

Katherine Ahern

HANDMADE LAMPS AND LAMPSHADES
KATHERINE AHERN

Martin Berinstein

Martin Berinstein

stacked-stone lamp

THE SPECIAL JOY OF THIS LAMP comes from its spontaneity. The ragged edges and imperfect stone surfaces are reminiscent of rocky outcroppings in far-distant, craggy landscapes. Cairnlike in appearance, this friendly beacon is as functional as it is beautiful.

MATERIALS

Sandstone or slate

Threaded brass rod (available at lighting stores)

Light socket

Harp sized appropriately for lamp base

Washer and nut

Electrical wire

Quick-setting epoxy

Lampshade

EQUIPMENT

Chalk

Tile-cutting saw

Scrap lumber

Drill with ⅜-inch (1 cm) concrete bit

Acrylic high-gloss spray (optional)

Hacksaw

Wire strippers or knife (optional)

Screwdriver

Felt or cork furniture protector tabs

Cutting and Drilling the Stone

1. Use chalk to rough out a cutting plan on the slab of stone. Because pieces will be irregular, accuracy is not important.

2. With the tile-cutting saw, cut slate or sandstone into twelve to fifteen irregular shapes of similar size that will be used for the lamp body.

3. Set a stone on a piece of scrap lumber. One at a time, drill a vertical hole through the center of each stone piece. Wash the sediment from each stone as you work.

4. For the base, choose a piece of stone, approximately 5 inches (12.5 cm) square, that has a flat, level side. Cut in half diagonally. Set these triangular pieces aside until it is time to attach the lamp base.

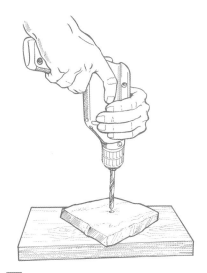

3 *Drill a vertical hole through the center of each stone.*

4 *Cut a piece of square, flat stone in half diagonally for the base.*

project continues on page 84 ▶

Assembling the Lamp Body

5. Stack the drilled stones one on top of another. Compare the height of the threaded rod to the height of the stacked stones. Using the hacksaw, cut the threaded rod so it is ¾-inch (1.9 cm) longer than the stacked stones are high.

6. Screw the light socket onto the end of the threaded rod, invert, and slide the harp support onto the rod so it is flush with the socket.

7. With the rod still inverted, begin threading the stones onto the rod. Place stones from small to large, always leading with the best side of the stone, which will then be visible when the lamp is turned upright. Secure the stone stack with a washer and a nut.

TIP: To give the stones an appealing, wet look, spray with a glossy acrylic finish before threading them onto the rod.

8. From the bottom of the lamp, thread the electrical wire up through the metal rod and out the top of the light socket. If the end of the electrical wire is coated in plastic, carefully strip off the last inch with wire strippers or a knife.

9. With screwdriver, loosen screws on either side of the light socket. Wrap exposed electrical wires around each screw. Secure screws well with screwdriver, ensuring good electrical contact.

10. Gently tug electrical wire at base of lamp to remove any slack.

Attaching the Lamp Base

11. Apply felt furniture protectors to the bottom of the two triangular base pieces.

12. Position the two base pieces so that their longest sides are next to and parallel to each other, leaving a small gap between.

13. Set the lamp body on top of the base pieces, thread the electrical cord through the gap between them to the back of the lamp, and slide the base pieces snug around the nut at the base of the threaded rod. Epoxy base pieces in place.

14. Insert a lightbulb, and top with a lampshade.

Fountain Variation

The same basic construction method can be used to make an inviting water fountain. Simply install pump tubing through the threaded rod, conceal the pump in a fountain bowl with a random arrangement of stones, and set the stacked-stone assembly on top. Follow manufacturer's instructions to install the re-circulating pump, and voilà. Water will spill down over the jagged surfaces into a pool below, creating a symphony of trickling water.

6 *Slide the harp support flush with socket.*

7 *Thread the stones onto the rod.*

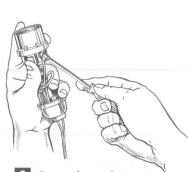

9 *Secure electrical wires in place with screwdriver.*

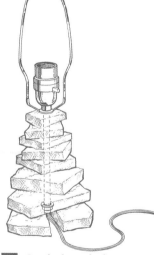

13 *Set the lamp body on top of base.*

paper and stone

Incandescent lighting can be made softer and more inviting when diffused through paper. Handmade papers are immensely popular, and the varieties and types of papers available can satisfy any taste. Some papers are fashioned with organic materials, natural fibers, mosses, and other fine textural additives. The translucence of rice paper imparts a bright yet subdued light, whereas other, heavier handmade papers contain the light within, casting their hues in rich display. The soft, muted tones of vegetable dyes contrast sharply with the brilliant, saturated color of commercial dyes.

Whether you wish to cover a lampshade form with paper, buy a shade, or fashion a unique shade of your own, try to tailor the shade's shape to suit a particular base. When choosing a paper for use as a shade, hold the paper up to direct light so you can see what the shade will look like when illuminated.

Caution: A shade fit snugly to a lightbulb is a potential fire hazard. When making a lampshade from paper, consider using low-watt lightbulbs for safety sake.

Combine the visual strength and integrity of a vertical stone column with the delicate, ethereal quality of a rice-paper lampshade for this trompe l'oeil lamp. Though there is no lighting fixture in the stone base, the proximity of the hanging shade to the stone creates the dramatic appearance of a sophisticated table lamp.

6

I saw the angel in the marble and carved
until I set him free.

—Michelangelo

Like people, rocks are unique. They possess a character, shape, color, and energy all their own. Some rocks speak to us, suggesting that they must become more than they appear to be.

Look at your stones. Determine how you can best bring forth their essence, their spirit. Some stones might have an in-

spirited stones
DISCOVERING THE POWER OF STONE

credible texture that demands to be touched. Others may be shaped in such a way that they suggest another form entirely. Still others might seem to be the proverbial tabula rasa, a blank slate awaiting our input and direction.

Let your stones inspire you. Awaken their hidden potential. Their spirit will speak to you. Their energy will fill you. Find joy in their simple presence.

WHAT IS *INUKSUK?*

Inuksuk ("ee-nook-shook") is an Inuit word that means "a thing that can act in place of a human being." For thousands of years, these structures of balanced rock have endured the extreme conditions of the Arctic, unflinching and ever-poised for duty. Often resembling human forms or set as small towers and columns of stone, *inuksuit* ("ee-nook-sweet," plural form of *inuksuk)* were used by the Inuit people to mark the land for myriad purposes. *Inuksuit* warned of danger, indicated a direction to follow, and recorded where food was stored, especially when under snow. They memorialized significant occurrences and celebrated the beauty of the land, erected as tokens of joy. And they were and are unwavering, ready helpers, forever directing caribou down paths where Inuit hunters lay in wait. *Inuksuit* bear witness to the strength of the Inuit people, who live and flourish in the vast, harsh, yet infinitely beautiful Arctic landscape.

Although cairns — piles of stones, often conical in shape, that are used as boundary markers, memorials, and burial sites — have been erected in other countries and cultures throughout the world, over time many have been damaged or dismantled, making the stalwart, ancient, lichen-covered survivors in the Arctic all the more exceptional. (For more information, consult Recommended Reading, page 148.)

Inspired by these magnificent creations, some people have started incorporating scaled-down versions of *inuksuit* in their gardens and homes. The structures can be large or small and configured any way you wish. The positioning of the stones is dictated mainly by their shape, and construction tends to be a trial-and-error process; balance is key. Traditionally, stones are balanced one atop another, but if your contemporary *inuksuk* will share space with children or pets, it's best to cement or wire the form together.

If you wish, re-create the look of ancient *inuksuk* by selecting lichen-covered stones and fashioning a small garden backdrop featuring plants in a scale typical of the Arctic tundra.

Brought indoors and positioned individually, these stone assemblages quickly become focal points for peaceful reflection.

Carin overlooking Floro Bay in Norway. Inuksuk are of a similar size and scale, but Inuit compositions are distinguished by their permanence and deliberate, purposeful construction.

indoor *inuksuk*

GATHERED ROCKS ARE BALANCED STRATEGICALLY to create intriguing stone assemblages, each one unique in appearance and personality. They stand silent and steadfast, waiting. This project features the human form, one of the more difficult structures to assemble. Patience and balance are key when undertaking this project. Before you begin, decide where the *inuksuk* will be displayed; this project must be assembled on site.

MATERIALS

Flat rocks

Blocklike rocks

Round rocks

Small stones

1. Gather a variety of rocks that are proportionate in size. In addition, choose some small stones that will be used to help buttress the structure.

TIP: When constructing the inuk-suk, *use small pebbles as shims to help position larger rocks and keep them in place. They can be used for support and to level uneven stones. For this project, good balance is the glue.*

2. Choose a flat rock for the base and place it on the work surface.

3. Choose two blocklike rocks of similar size and shape for the legs. Position them vertically on the base. Lay a flat rock across the tops of the legs to form the hips.

4. Select a blocklike rock for the torso and place it next.

5. Choose an extra-long flat rock or two smaller flat rocks for the arms. Position so rock extends beyond the width of the torso.

6. Center a large round rock atop the figure. If two rocks were used to make the arms, carefully hold them in place while positioning this last rock.

Make a simple inuksuk *with round stones secured in place with putty.*

PICTURE STONES

HUNDREDS OF thousands of years ago, indigenous peoples inscribed and painted symbols and pictures on rock to record and communicate information. Though the origins of this work remain largely unexplained, we marvel at the ways primitive peoples told stories and identified battlegrounds, significant occurrences, and environmental change.

The term *petroglyph* describes images and symbols that are carved and inscribed into a rock surface, likely with smaller rocks. *Pictograph,* though similar, refers to images that are painted on rocks with natural dyes and pigments. Over time, harsh elements have eroded the surfaces of many petroglyphs, marring the definition of the original carvings. Interestingly, the coloration of many pictographs has been preserved and remains quite distinct. When rain falls, the water washes the rock's mineral content over the paintings, sealing and protecting them from the elements.

petroglyphs and pictographs

FIND AN INTERESTING ROCK THAT SPEAKS TO YOU in some way and create your own petroglyph or pictograph. Use traditional symbols or stylize your design to capture today's contemporary spirit. Display your modern artifacts on twig easels, in shadowbox frames, or propped up against other rocks in interesting groupings. To learn more about some contemporary glyphs and their meanings, see the discussion of totems on page 107.

To learn more about some contemporary glyphs and their meanings, see the discussion of totems on page 107.

MATERIALS

FOR PETROGLYPH:
Soft rock (like sandstone or slate) with a relatively smooth surface

FOR PICTOGRAPH:
Flat rock

EQUIPMENT

FOR PETROGLYPH:
Pencil
Rotary tool with assorted grinding bits
Toothbrush
Paint, acrylic or enamel (optional)
Paintbrush, fine (optional)

FOR PICTOGRAPH:
Pencil
Indelible ink marker
Paint, acrylic or enamel (optional)
Paintbrush, fine (optional)
Gold metallic liquid marker (optional)
Protective spray sealer (optional)

PETROGLYPH

1. Wash the stone well and let dry.

2. With the pencil, draw the outline of the symbol you wish to inscribe on the stone's surface. Keep the design simple.

3. Using the rotary tool and a grinding bit appropriate to the size of the symbol you have chosen, grind away the stone *within* the outline, as shown below. If you wish, vary the depth of the design for greater detail. Simply apply added pressure to the grinding tool where you wish to grind away more stone, or work the tool over an area repeatedly.

4. Clean the carving with a toothbrush, thoroughly removing any rock dust.

5. Leave the carving as is for a natural look. To accentuate the design, paint either the carved surface or the uncarved surface of the rock.

PICTOGRAPH

1. Wash the stone well and let dry.

2. On the stone's surface, outline in pencil the shape of the symbol you have chosen.

3. Trace the outline with indelible ink or paint, as shown at right, and fill with color. Let dry.

4. Trace the symbol's outline with metallic marker, if desired.

5. If you'll display the pictograph indoors, nothing further is needed. If you'll display it outdoors, however, a coating of protective spray sealer is strongly recommended.

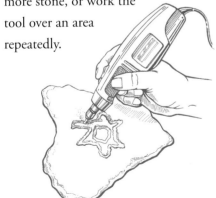

3 *For the petroglyph, grind away the stone within the outline.*

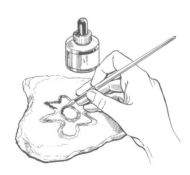

3 *For the pictograph, trace the outline with ink or paint.*

decorative cement stones

Cement and stone are weighty, durable, and strong. This project uses each to great advantage. Use pebbles, shells, glass, and other textural elements to make a sophisticated or simple design. Display decorative stones in the garden as stepping stones or inside your home as contemporary artifacts. Use flat stones to hold groupings of candles or as exotic displays for handmade soaps in the bathroom. Decorative stones make excellent gifts and cherished keepsakes, and are wonderful objects for quiet contemplation.

The following instructions are for a 12-inch-square (30 cm) decorative cement stone.

MATERIALS

30" (75 cm) piece of 1 x 12 spruce roofing board

1½" (3.8) nails

Stones and pebbles

Shells, glass jewels, and other embellishments (optional)

Fast-set cement

Water

Cement sealer (optional)

EQUIPMENT

Saw

Ruler/measuring tape

Pencil

Hammer

Newspaper

Plastic wrap

Pail

Plastic scoop

Large stick to stir cement

Disposable plastic food tub

Paper towels

Wood Mold

1. Cut a 12-inch (30 cm) length from the board, which will serve as the mold's base.

2. Cut the remaining board lengthwise in four strips approximately 3 inches (7.5 cm) wide. These are the mold's side pieces.

3. Cut two side pieces to 12-inch (30 cm) lengths.

4. Nail the 12-inch (30 cm) sides to the base, opposite each other.

5. Nail the remaining two sides in place, as shown, and place the mold on several sheets of newspaper.

TIP: For easy mold removal, don't hammer the nails completely flush with the wood on one side. Leave the nail heads up just enough for easy hammer-claw access. When the decorative cement stone has dried completely, you'll rely on plastic wrap to help remove the stone. If the stone is difficult to lift out, even with plastic wrap, remove the side from the mold and the stone should lift out more easily.

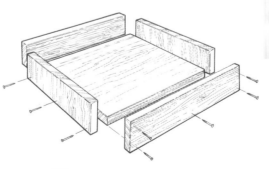

5 *Nail sides to base.*

project continues on page 96 ▶

6. Lay a sheet of plastic wrap over the wood mold so that it hangs over the side pieces. You may need to lay one sheet of plastic wrap horizontally across the mold and one sheet vertically to ensure sufficient coverage.

Design Template

7. Cut a 12-inch square (30 cm) piece of paper and set it beside the mold.

8. On the paper template, experiment with a selection of stones, pebbles, shells, and other embellishments until you come up with a pattern that you'd like to use on the cement stone. Be sure that all embellishments are right side up and as you'd like them to appear in the finished stone.

Molding the Stone

9. Prepare the cement in a pail following the manufacturer's instructions. Alternate additions of dry cement and water, and use a large stick to stir the cement well after each addition. Working incrementally like this will give you greater control. The cement is ready when its consistency is thick but can still be poured.

10. Scoop the cement into a disposable plastic food tub and then pour onto the plastic wrap in the mold as shown at right. Fill the mold almost to the top. Gently shift the container from side to side, leveling the cement and filling the corners fully; this also removes air bubbles.

11. Working quickly, begin transferring your decorative pattern from the template to the wet cement. Press pieces firmly into the cement as you place them. If excess water begins accumulating at the top of the mold, dab the mold with paper towels until the water is absorbed. Let mold air-dry for 24 hours.

12. Place your hand across the front of the mold and carefully invert the mold. Tug the plastic wrap gently to assist in removal of the stone. If the stone is stubborn, remove the nails from one side of the mold, remove the side, and again attempt to remove the stone. The stone is extremely fragile at this point, so be careful.

13. Allow the stone to air-dry completely for a week. You'll notice the edges of the stone lightening in color as it dries, but because it's not exposed to the air it takes the inside even longer to dry.

14. Seal the stone with brush-on cement sealer, if desired. If you plan to use your stone outdoors, this step is strongly recommended.

Variation

Make decorative stones of different shapes and sizes by using aluminum or tin pie plates with steep sides for molds. No plastic wrap is needed when using aluminum or tin. Pie plates are great time-savers if you plan to make many decorative stones in one sitting.

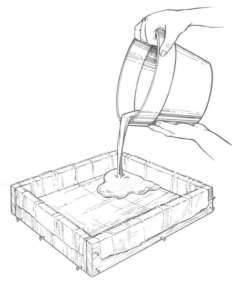

10 *Pour cement into the mold.*

11 *Place and press pieces into the cement.*

TRADITIONAL DRY-LANDSCAPE GARDENS

OR CENTURIES, dry-landscape gardens were maintained in Japan, but not until the eleventh century did they begin to evolve. At that time, Zen priests began adopting dry gardens to cultivate understanding of Zen principles and to foster deeper meditation and contemplation. The best known and most photographed garden of this type in Japan is Ryoan-ji in Kyoto — referred to by some as "the garden of nothingness."

Through Zen philosophy, we can experience the large in the small. In the dry-landscape garden, large rocks represent mountains and islands, and crushed granite flowing water — auspicious elements for contemplation. The crushed stones are raked in endless patterns — straight and circular paths — evoking a sense of the ebb and flow of the ocean tide and meandering rivers. In Japanese culture, islands represent longevity and good health.

A dry garden is not entered, but viewed; truly, it is a garden of the mind. Creating, maintaining, and contemplating such a garden brings profound peace.

"The garden of nothingness" at Ryoan-ji in Kyoto, Japan, is meticulously maintained. Raking is an opportunity for profound meditation.

tabletop zen garden

MATERIALS

Garden container, approximately 12"x12" (30 x 30 cm)

Twig, approximately 1" (2.5 cm) thick

Few tiny branches

White sand

Rocks, suitably sized for garden

EQUIPMENT

Pruning shears

Sharp utility knife (optional)

Tenon, ½" (1 cm) (optional)

Drill (drill press is best) with ½" (1 cm) and ³⁄₁₆" (5 mm) bits

Pen

Wood glue

THIS TABLETOP VERSION OF THE ZEN GARDEN encourages us to nudge our busy minds into a peaceful, contemplative place. With sand and stone, we bring the earth's basic elements into our living space.

Sitting, relaxed and comfortable, you will draw the rake's tines through the sand, inscribing patterns around the stones, making a perfect path, without beginning or end. It's a relaxing, therapeutic process that can refresh you after a busy day. Enjoy working in this thought-filled garden, rain or shine.

Making the Rake

1. With pruning shears, cut the twig to a length of approximately 10 inches (25 cm) for the rake handle.

2. With pruning shears or a sharp knife, pare one end of the handle down to ½ inch (1.3 cm) in diameter. If using a tenon, insert one end of the handle into the tenon, reducing it to the desired ½-inch (1.3 cm) diameter.

3. To discourage the bark from peeling, trim the top edge of the opposite end with pruning shears, keeping them at a constant 45-degree angle. Alternatively, use sandpaper to strike vertically at the end of the handle. Set aside.

4. Cut the remaining twig to a length of approximately 2¾ inches (6.9 cm) for the rake head. Trim the ends to keep bark from peeling.

5. In the center of the rake head, drill a hole for the twig handle with the ½-inch (1.3 cm) bit, being careful not to exceed half the twig depth.

6. Rotate the rake head so that the holes for the tines can be positioned at about 120 degrees from the handle. With a pen, mark five or six evenly spaced dots on the rake head. Drill holes for the tines with the ³⁄₁₆-inch (5 mm) bit, being careful not to exceed half the twig depth.

7. Secure rake handle into rake head with wood glue.

8. Pare down ends of tines, if necessary, to ensure a snug fit. Remove tines from holes, one at a time, glue ends, and replace. Let dry. Trim tine ends with pruning shears, leaving them an even inch (2.5 cm) long.

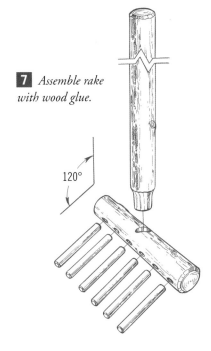

7 *Assemble rake with wood glue.*

120°

project continues on page 100 ▶

Creating the Garden

9. Fill the garden base halfway with dry sand.

TIP: If you use sand from a plastic bag, it's likely the sand is holding some moisture. For best results, allow the sand to dry completely before attempting to rake it.

10. Add rocks to the garden one by one, spacing them well apart. If you wish, use only one or two rocks. Stack them. Change them. Experiment. Play.

11. With a relaxed wrist and using light pressure, draw the rake *slowly* from the garden's outside edges into the garden, or around the rocks and outward. You should be able to move the rake freely around the garden, with no interference from the container sides or the rocks. If you can't do so, you have used too many rocks, the rocks are too large, or they're placed too closely together.

12. Rake slowly in a continuous pattern, retracing your lines, in an attempt to create a perfectly flowing design.

In traditional dry-style gardens large rocks represent mountains and islands, and crushed granite flowing water.

Traditional dry-style garden at Tofuku-ji in Kyoto, Japan

LIKE MANY PEOPLE WHO JUDGE THEIR ARTISTIC ABILITIES
solely on whether or not they can draw, early on Mark Richardson discounted his
creative talents. But less than a decade ago, he discovered his perfect medium: sandblasting. In sandblasting, a stream of sand is projected through a tip by compressed
air, the stone beneath melting away, as if in slow motion, leaving behind a precise,
incised image. The sandblaster's craft requires skill, patience, and a steady hand.

Mark's early work consisted of engravings on flat stone monuments. But soon
he began working with natural found stones. He chooses each stone carefully, rely-
ing on logic, intuition, and an interview of sorts to determine how the stone will be
used. Obviously, the stone must be large enough to accommodate the design

SANDBLASTED STONE

MARK RICHARDSON

layout, but it also must *feel* right for the job. Mark carefully handles and scrutinizes
each stone. Some stones lack structural integrity and have other inconsistencies
that can devastate a piece. Then Mark asks the stone if it is right for the job and lis-
tens for its response.

Mark creates a rubber stencil for each design with a computer-controlled cutter,
then adheres the stencil to the prepared rock face. Stencils improve control, result-
ing in crisp uniform letters and images.

Mark also creates functional bowls or "cores" in natural rock by sandblasting
freehand. Examples of this work can be found on pages 52 and 70.

Mark's business, Marked in Stone, has an international clientele and accepts
commissions for projects ranging from address and garden stones to company logos.

7. When you find the perfect spot for the spout, remove the driftwood from the bowl, and drill a hole up through the underside of the wood. Remember, the hole will be straight when drilled.

8. Thread the plastic tubing through the drilled hole, and reposition the driftwood in the bowl.

9. Arrange rocks in the bowl for a visually and audibly pleasing result. Slight adjustments in stone placement and the number of stones used will alter the sound of the falling water considerably. Experiment until you're happy with the result.

10. Fill bowl to within 1 inch (2.5 cm) of the top with distilled water.

Fountain Maintenance

- Never allow the water level to drop so low that it exposes the pump. Insufficient water level can damage the pump. Add distilled water when necessary.

- To ensure smooth operation of the pump, run the fountain for extended periods, rather than turning it on and off frequently.

- Disassemble the fountain from time to time, then scrub components in soapy water. Soak the pump in a 50/50 vinegar and water bath for ten minutes to remove any mineral build-up.

- Unplug the fountain if you will be away for several days to avoid damage to pump that may be caused by an insufficient water level.

Place the fountain to best advantage. Here, an amaryllis is positioned behind the fountain, giving the composition dramatic height and visual interest.

ANIMAL TOTEMS

ERIVED FROM NATIVE American and Celtic cultures, animal totems are mystical symbols that represent important lessons on our journeys through life. In these early cultures, animals were highly revered, and it was believed that divine forces communicated important lessons, to guide and protect, through animal spirits. These lessons are sometimes designated as *animal medicine*, "medicine" referring to energy in the form of a vital life force. Today, animal medicine can teach us to acknowledge and heal flaws in our personalities and thinking that may block our progress on life's path.

Animal totems, when inscribed on stones, allow us to carry with us symbols of the animals whose medicine we need. Some believe that the medicine we need is revealed to us through dreams, meditations, or unexpected sightings or heightened interest in a particular animal.

Review the listing of animals and primary lessons in the chart. Keep in mind that all totems have equally important messages to convey to us. (See Recommended Reading on page 148 for more information on animal totems.)

Key to Animal Totems*

Animal	Lesson	Animal	Lesson
Armadillo	Boundaries	Hummingbird	Joy, optimism
Bat	Rebirth, release fear	Lizard	Dreaming, conservation
Bear	Introspection, power within	Moose	Self-esteem, integrity
Bear paw	Power, direction	Mountain lion	Leadership
Beaver	Builder, gatherer	Mouse	Scrutiny
Buffalo	Prayer, abundance, sacredness	Otter	Feminine power, fun-seeking
Butterfly	Transformation	Owl	Wisdom, patience, truth
Canada goose	Sacred circle	Peacock	Wholeness
Cat	Wholeness	Rabbit	Fear, alertness
Cougar	Courage, power	Raccoon	Dexterity, disguise
Coyote	Trickster	Raven	Trickster, hoarder, teacher
Crane	Solitude, independence	Robin	Growth, renewal
Deer	Gentleness, sensitivity	Salamander	Transformation
Dolphin	Breath of life, kindness	Salmon	Instinct, persistence, wisdom
Dragonfly	Illusion, carefree	Seal	Inner voice
Eagle	Spirit	Skunk	Self-respect
Elephant	Commitment	Snake	Transmutation, fertility
Elk	Stamina, strength	Spider	Weaver, creativity
Fox	Intelligence, provider, camouflage	Squirrel	Gathering
Frog	Healing, water	Swan	Grace, innocence
Hawk	Messenger, observer	Turtle	Mother Earth, adaptable
Horse	Power, mobility, strength	Whale	Record keeper
		Wolf	Teacher, loyalty, stability

* To yield greatest benefit, study the animal. For example, the beaver represents building and gathering, but it is also symbolic of emotions and dreams. Beavers mate for life, build intricate homes, and are family oriented. Skill and dedication to work and family define the beaver.

animal totems

TOTEM STONES CAN SERVE AS IMPORTANT reminders and touchstones in our daily lives. They possess a mystical spiritual power, working as teachers, protectors, and healers. Consult the Key to Animal Totems on page 107 to learn more about a particular animal.

It is believed that stones take with them the energies of their origins, so choose stones from places having the energy you want. For example, choose stones from a rugged ocean coastline if you wish to harness the unbridled power of crashing waves, or from a trickling forest stream to gain the tranquility of a peaceful woodland setting.

Be aware that stones with sandblasted totem symbols are widely available at gift shops and New Age and healing arts centers. Occasionally, the word representing the totem is used on the stone so the medicine required is clear.

MATERIALS

Small stones

EQUIPMENT

Pencil

Stencils (optional)

Spray adhesive

Paintbrush, fine

India ink

Indelible markers

Paint, acrylic or enamel

Clear spray sealer (optional)

1. Collect smooth, small stones.

2. Wash stones well and let them air-dry completely.

3. With a pencil, sketch on the center of the rock the outline of the totem you've chosen. Alternatively, apply a small stencil to the rock with spray adhesive.

4. In a medium of your choice, color the image. If a stencil was used to create the image, remove. Let dry.

5. Finish with a coat of spray sealer, if you wish.

Sandblasted totems like these can be found at gift shops and at New Age and healing arts centers.

RUNIC CHARACTERS

I

T IS UNCLEAR when runic characters originated, but many accounts date them to the third century when they were used by the Germanic and Nordic peoples. In the sixth through twelfth centuries, runic characters were used extensively by Vikings as talismans on their wooden ships.

Runic symbols were carved into pieces of wood, stone, leather, and bone. They served as a means of communication and were believed to hold divining properties. Historically, rune stones have been used as talismans and for healing, protection, interpretation of omens, and to clarify issues that may muddy the vision and purpose of one's life path.

There are twenty-four runic characters in the alphabet, but a blank stone has been added to represent the unknown. Each of the runic characters has a unique symbolic meaning. Runes are laid out in a specific pattern in preparation for a reading. Readings involve analysis of the symbols of the stones, and predictions and observations are made based on individual and combined meanings of the stones. Not unlike tarot cards, rune stones are chisels and picks used to excavate deeply buried personal issues and their possible solutions.

Each day, randomly select one rune stone and reflect on its meaning. Over time, you will become familiar with each stone while contemplating the wisdom it brings forth. In addition to the meanings given in the chart below, many other associations can be made for each runic symbol. See Recommended Reading on page 148 for more information.

Runes and Their Meanings

Rune	Symbol	Meaning
Ur ("er")	ᚢ	New beginnings, advancement, wellness
Thurs ("thers")	ᚦ	Strength, power, energy
Ass ("ace")	ᚨ	Inspiration, communication, wisdom
Reid ("ride")	ᚱ	Journeying, direction, motion
Ken ("ken")	ᚲ	Intellect, guidance, creative fire
Gifu ("gee-foo")	ᚷ	Generosity, gifts, love
Wynja ("win-yah")	ᚹ	Joy, happiness, success
Hagal ("har-gool")	ᚺ or ᚼ	Change, setbacks
Naud ("need")	ᚾ	Need, necessity, caution
Iss ("ees")	ᛁ	Ice, coldness, delay, waiting
Jara ("yah-rah")	ᛃ	Year, natural cycle, timing
Pertra ("pert-rah")	ᛈ	Recollection, advance, acceptance
Eoh ("yo")	ᛇ	Yew tree, motivation, durability, completion
Algiz ("all-giz")	ᛉ	Instinctive, protection
Sol ("sole")	ᛋ or ᛌ	Sun, healing, good health, rejuvenation
Tyr ("tire")	ᛏ	Courage, honesty, trust
Bjarka ("beyarkah")	ᛒ	Family, growth, nurturing, culture
Eh ("eh")	ᛗ	Cooperation, progress, change
Madr ("marder")	ᛙ	Uniqueness, comprehension, attitude
Lagu ("largoo")	ᛚ	Intuition, emotions, unconscious
Ing ("ing")	◇ or ᛝ	Fertility, completion, fulfillment
Odal ("owed-all")	ᛟ	Home, property, culture
Dagaz ("dargaz")	ᛞ	Change, awakening, new day
Feh ("fe")	ᚠ	Success, fortune, abundance
"Blank"		Destiny, unknown, faith, wish

rune stones

MATERIALS

25 Small elongated, flat, smooth stones

Indelible marker

Paint, acrylic or enamel

EQUIPMENT

Paintbrush

Rotary tool (optional)

WITH THE RENEWED INTEREST IN RUNES in our modern-day quest to discover our authentic selves, runes are fairly easy to obtain. However, the best runes are those that you make yourself from materials of your choosing. These runes are infused with your energy from the start. Study and learn the meanings of the runic characters as you create your rune stones.

1. Select twenty-five smooth stones that you can hold in the palm of your hand at once. Runes are often interpreted differently when they are inverted, so choose stones that are somewhat elongated.

2. Working on each stone's flattest side, draw a single runic character onto the stone, leaving one stone blank. Use indelible inks, paint, or etch the symbols with a rotary tool. The latter requires a fairly soft stone such as soapstone or sandstone.

3. Many rune books offer rituals that can be performed prior to working with the stones to activate them and fill them with life force. See Recommended Reading on page 148 for more information.

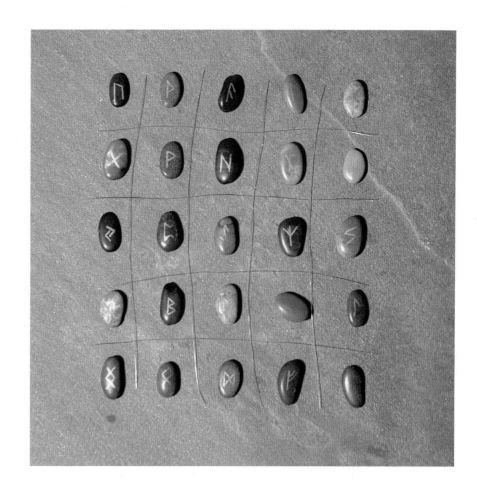

7

From the earliest age, stone has been used to decorate and adorn. Precious and semiprecious gemstones and stunning crystals are mainstays of the jewelers' craft, precision-cut into multifaceted works of art to be treasured through the years.

Cherished is the jewelry that passes down through the generations, from grandmother to granddaughter, father to son. Although we can appreciate the skill and craftsmanship that has

stylish stones
ADORNING YOURSELF WITH STONE

gone into their making, it's the emotional ties to the people who wore them that bind us to these pieces. Jewelry has a vitality beyond its value and beauty; it has a spirit all its own.

Common, found stones also have great potential when fashioned into wearable art, particularly when the stones themselves have sentimental value, recalling a special place or time. The stones need not be extraordinary. Even a humble stone can be transformed into a stunning accessory. Delight in its simple beauty.

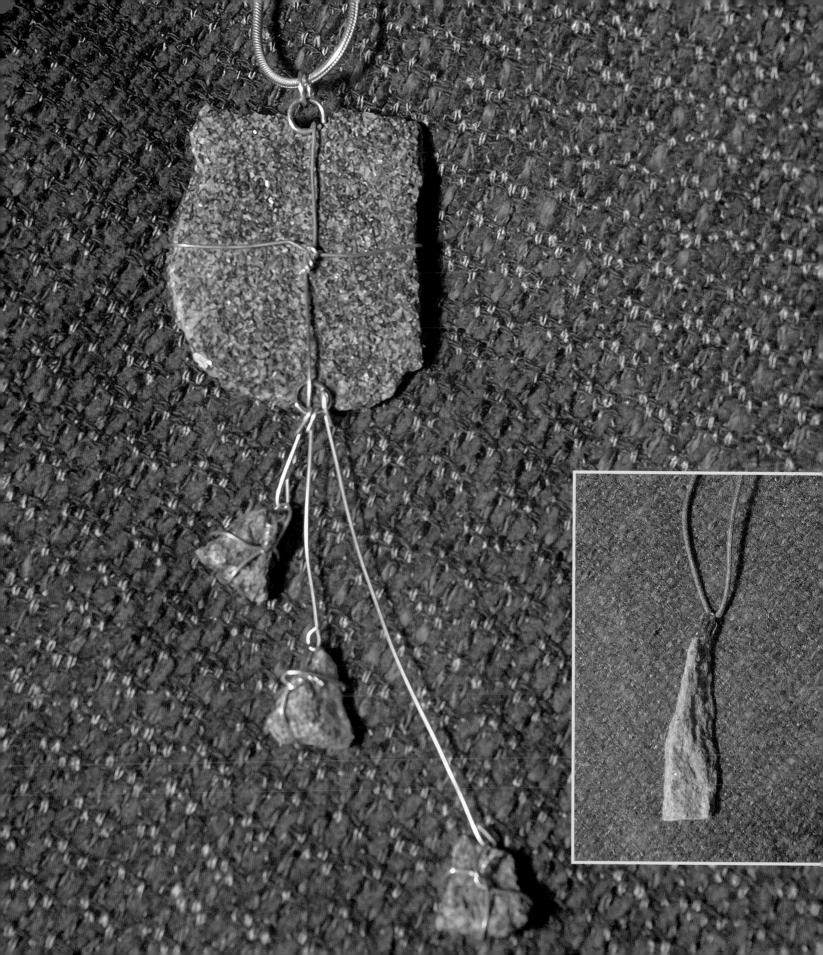

stone pendant

EVERY NOW AND THEN, a small stone will speak to you in such a way that you're compelled to keep it with you. What better way to celebrate the spirit of that stone than in a piece of jewelry? Pendants and brooches make excellent homes for found stones. And the basic techniques are simple.

Pendants are traditionally made with gemstones and crystals, but simple stone pendants can be equally beautiful. Begin with a roughly textured stone for your first piece, as smooth stones can be slippery and difficult to work with. These pieces make great gifts and cherished mementos, particularly when the stone holds special meaning for the recipient. If you find a stone that's a real "gem," consider commissioning a professional jeweler to mount it for you.

MATERIALS

Small textured stone

Silver, copper, or brass wire, any pliable gauge

Jump ring

Chain or cord

EQUIPMENT

Needle-nose pliers

Wire cutters

1. Use fine wire to enfold the stone. Wrap the stone in a functional, aesthetically pleasing configuration, keeping wire ends at the back. For example, crossing wire from side to side and end to end holds a square stone securely.

2. With needle-nose pliers, twist the ends of the wire around themselves to tighten. Snip excess wire and press ends flush with stone.

3. Attach a jump ring to the top of the pendant, under the wrapped wire, or fashion a small wire loop at the top of the pendant.

4. Measure a cord, or choose a chain, that suspends the pendant at an appropriate level. The cord or chain should be proportionate to the size and style of the pendant and the wearer. Thread through the jump ring.

TIP: Leather and rattail cording, leather lacing, and metal chains are available at craft stores and jewelry suppliers. All are excellent ways to hang a pendant. Choose the one you like best.

Embellishments

5. If you wish, add a few dangling pebbles to the pendant. Simply wrap tiny stones in wire as previously described.

6. Cut wire to desirable lengths for extensions.

7. Thread the end of each wire extension through wrapped wire on pendant and, with pliers, bend ends over to secure.

8. Attach other end of wire extension to wrapped wire on tiny stone(s), and bend ends over to secure.

Left, inset: *For a spare design and a quick alternative to this approach, secure a star-shaped jewelry fitting to a stone with quick-setting epoxy or superglue. Finish with a jump ring and cord or chain.*

decorative jewelry

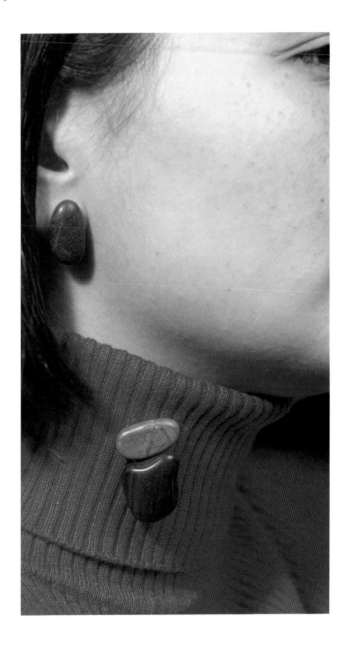

If you're like me, your first successful jewelry-making effort might inspire you to make something else — a more complex, decorative piece, perhaps. Read a few jewelry-making books to learn basic techniques and to get some design ideas, then get started (See Recommended Reading on page 148 for more information.)

River rocks are smoothed to perfection by rushing water. Small polished pebbles are lightweight and ideal for earthy, natural, understated jewelry.

For earrings, choose pebbles that are an appealing color and of similar shape and size. For a brooch, select stones of complementary or contrasting colors that fit well together physically. Place stones good-side down on the work surface. With superglue or quick-setting epoxy, adhere earring posts and a brooch pin to the backs of the stones. Allow to set until completely dry.

Polishing Your Own Stones

If you want to use something other than naturally polished stones for your jewelry, you can polish your own. Beginner's rock-tumbling kits are available at most hobby shops, and professional-grade tumblers are available at specialty stores. Rock tumblers strive to mimic the ocean's natural tumbling action. Clean rocks of similar hardness are placed in the rubber-lined tumbler barrel, with carefully graded abrasive materials and water. The tumbler agitates the materials. In just a few weeks, the rock tumbler produces what it takes Mother Nature years to accomplish — beautifully polished stones.

Left: *Sophisticated and appealing, this copper bracelet was hand forged. The subtle texture was achieved by striking the metal with the rounded end of a ballpeen hammer. The meandering metalwork design echoes the shape of the featured stone.*

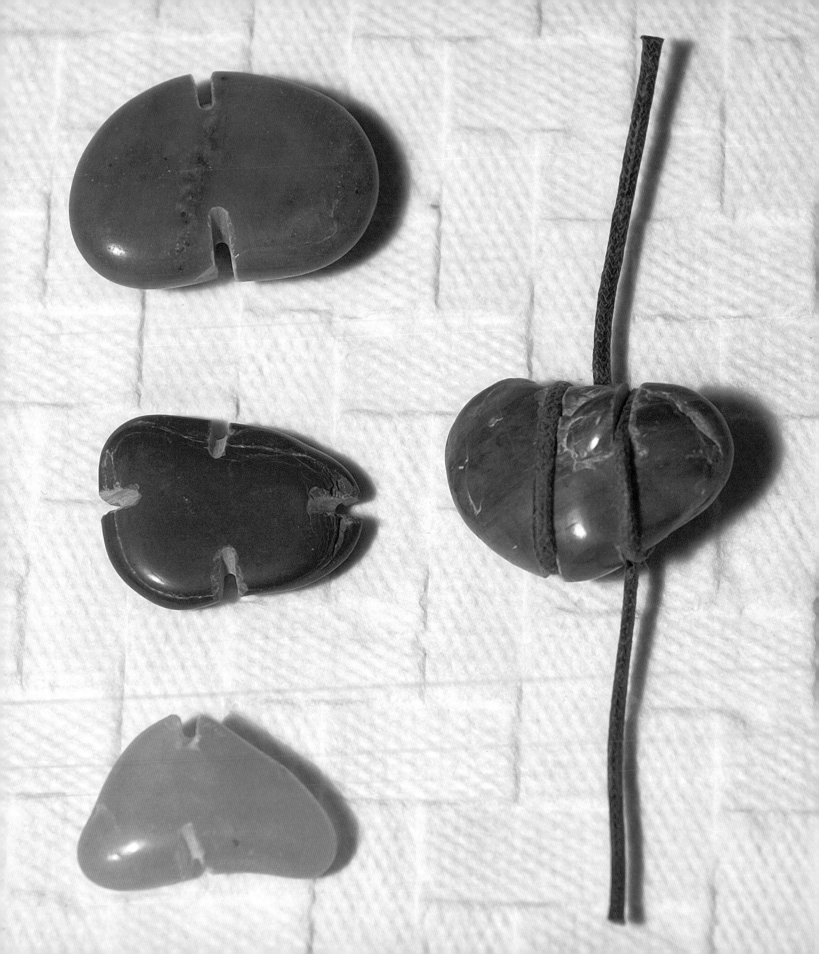

buttons

Years ago, I used to do leatherwork. I made purses, wallets, and jewelry bags from leather and trimmed them with beadwork. I loved the way a single bone button could add a delightful finishing touch to these pieces. If a project requires just one button as a closure, why not use something special?

Recalling some of these favorite projects inspired me to design buttons from stone. They're wonderful natural accents that complement any fabric.

MATERIALS

Small rounded stones
Cording, waxed or leather
Flat shale or sandstone

EQUIPMENT

Tile-cutting saw
Drill with ⅛" (3 mm) diamond bit

Round Buttons

1. Touch opposing edges of a stone against the blade of the tile-cutting saw to make small indents.

2. Wrap cording around the stone and fasten.

3. Experiment by making multiple indents on each side of the stone, which allow you to make different patterns with the cord.

Square Buttons

1. With the tile-cutting saw, cut the shale or sandstone piece to desired size.

2. Drill two or four holes for a traditional-looking button, or drill additional holes to accommodate decorative lacing.

3. Secure button with cording.

A round natural-stone button accentuates the beauty of woven wool.

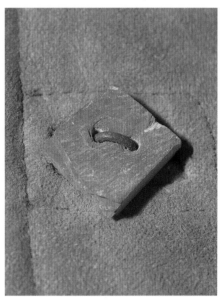

Shale secured with leather cording offers a textural counterpoint to soft, buff-colored suede.

LAURIE HEATH WAS A SERIOUS ROCK HOUND AS A CHILD, her passion indulged by her prospector grandfather whose extensive collection inspired and intrigued her. Her path to jewelry making was serendipitous, receiving jewelry-making supplies as a gift ten years ago. She incorporated beads, polymer clay, and gemstones in her early work.

Bit by the jewelry-making bug, in 1994 she began Ladybird Designs, making unique custom pieces and supplying shops with funky, one-of-a-kind jewelry shortly thereafter. Laurie's signature style of wire wrapping was born out of necessity; she found commercial jewelry findings (clasps, ear wires, etc.) stale, monotonous, and inappropriate for the pieces she envisioned.

STONE JEWELRY
LAURIE HEATH

Using mainly common hand tools, sterling silver, and sometimes a torch, Laurie works with the natural characteristics of each stone to arrive at a unique piece. Her study of ancient jewelry can often be recognized as an influence in her simple, detailed technique.

After being diagnosed with breast cancer in 1999, Laurie's perspective shifted. She abandoned what she now considers her inhibitions about design, allowing her style to evolve further. She believes that the experience of having cancer has granted her the freedom to create unhindered from a deeper source.

8

As humans, we delight in the unexpected: a clever turn of phrase, a giant pumpkin, a smiling stone. Surprise, disbelief, and humor are our greatest allies on the short but pleasant road to stone whimsy.

As you've done for past chapters, look at stones creatively, imagining what they might become and how you might use

stone whimsy
PLAYFUL USES FOR STONE

them playfully, in unusual, unexpected ways. The possibilities are nearly endless.

The projects that follow should serve as touchstones for your own creative efforts. Harness all the childlike wonder you can muster, and let the fun begin!

birdbath fountain

A CEMENT BIRDBATH BECOMES A STRIKING, unexpected feature when placed in an interior setting. Create a garden nook in your home and make this fountain its centerpiece, or place it in a foyer or hallway to welcome guests. The rock menagerie positioned in the bowl becomes the water's partner, encouraging it to dance and sing to the delight of all.

MATERIALS

Cement birdbath bowl and pedestal

Cement sealer

Collection of rocks (one drilled, optional)

Submergible recirculating water pump

Plastic tubing

Distilled water

EQUIPMENT

Paintbrush, 2" (5 cm)

Scissors

1. If the cement birdbath is new, fill it with water and observe it for 2 days, looking for cracks and leaks in the cement. If all is well, dump out water and let the bowl dry thoroughly. Do not use a cracked or leaking bowl for this project.

2. Brush the interior of the bowl with cement sealer. Let dry.

3. Place pump in the bowl, and arrange rocks to conceal it, leaving the tube fitting exposed for the time being. If using a drilled rock, thread the plastic tubing up through the hole and cut it so that it is long enough to stay in place in the rock and short enough not to be seen. Attach tubing to pump. If not using a drilled rock, stack rocks in a manner that will secure and conceal the tubing and pump, while allowing water to trickle gently down the rocks.

4. Run the pump's power cord behind the pedestal of the birdbath so it is hidden from view.

5. Add distilled water to the bowl to cover the pump. Fill bowl to within 2 inches (5 cm) of top or to suit the action and sound of your fountain. If using a drilled rock, you might need to drop a pebble into the hole to help diffuse the water and prevent it from spraying straight up into the air. *Note:* Pumps typically come equipped with regulators to adjust water flow. Experiment until you get the flow just right for your configuration.

TIP: Always use distilled water, as it prevents mineral deposits from developing.

6. Plug in the pump to test the water flow. Add or adjust rocks, if necessary, to improve the water flow and to enhance its trickling sound. Add more water to the birdbath bowl if needed.

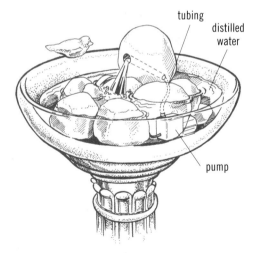

3 *Thread plastic tubing through drilled hole and attach to pump.*

water world

The textures and colors of stone are at their most vivid when wet. By constantly washing stones with water, indoor fountains help stones look their best. But there are other, quieter ways to observe stones in their water-washed state.

A glass container of any size and shape, when filled with water, offers an unmatched opportunity for viewing stones. Place a few favorite stones in a water-filled container. Add a goldfish or two, which can live quite happily in this impromptu habitat. Float candles on the surface. The eye is drawn alternately from the candles to the swimming fish, all the while studying the stony landscape. This water world offers a tremendous opportunity for quiet reflection.

Caution: Light floating candles only *after* they have been placed in water, and use long safety matches. Never leave a burning candle unattended.

stone critters

Often stone speaks quietly to us, insisting that it's something different, surprising us with its shape, and resembling something it simply cannot be. Or can it? A bird, a fish, a face — if only it had wings or fins or hair, everyone would know the secret longings of that stone. So why not help it along?

Depending on the stone's hardness, you might choose to drill small holes in it to help set its character free. Then insert feathers, shaped wire pieces, or perhaps small doll parts. If the rock is too hard to drill, use wire to attach embellishments to the stone. Children can have hours of fun creating stone friends and dressing them up with pipe cleaners, foam shapes, and virtually anything their hearts desire.

More sophisticated equipment can help you make strong, sturdy, weather-tolerant critters from stone and wrought iron, like these critters crafted by Dan Ansems of Belmont, Ontario. Animated stone friends make fun, whimsical additions to garden or patio. Of course, if you don't want to let your stone critters out of your sight, by all means keep them indoors.

pebble birdhouse

THIS QUAINT PEBBLE BIRDHOUSE features stonework reminiscent of English country cottages. The small stones for this project are easy to find and can be gathered almost anywhere. If you're fortunate to have a pebble or gravel driveway, start your search there.

Choose a wood base house appropriate for the birds you wish to attract. The house will appeal to finches, sparrows, chickadees, and possibly other birds that frequent your backyard.

MATERIALS

Wood birdhouse, any size or dimension

Acrylic paint

Kitchen tile grout compound, premixed

Small pebbles, 1" (2.5 cm) or less

Sand

White glue (optional)

Bark (optional)

Wood glue (optional)

Short nails (optional)

EQUIPMENT

Newspaper

Paintbrush

Putty knife or spreader

Spoon

Hammer (optional)

Staple gun (optional)

Preparing the House

1. Cover the work surface well with newspaper.

2. Using acrylic paint that complements or matches the color of the stones, paint the roof, back, perch, and any other surface of the birdhouse that won't be covered with pebbles. Let set one hour or until dry.

TIP: If the house will be mounted on a wall, the back of the house should be painted, not pebbled, so the house can rest flush. If the house will be freestanding, pebble the back as well.

Decorating the Sides

3. Using the putty knife, spread a smooth, generous layer of grout over one side of the house. To preserve moisture, keep a lid on the grout compound when not in use.

4. Randomly place some large pebbles in the grout, pressing them gently. Then place smaller pebbles, leaving slight spaces between the stones. Continue applying stones until the side is covered.

5. Using a spoon, collect some tiny pebbles and sand and sprinkle them over any spots where grout is still visible. Set the pebbles and sand in the grout with the back of the spoon or your finger. Let dry overnight.

6. Repeat steps 3–5 for the other two sides.

TIP: If you notice gaps in the stonework after the grout has dried, simply apply a bit of fresh grout or a dab of white glue to an appropriately sized stone and set it in place for a seamless fix.

project continues on page 130 ▶

Decorating the Front

7. With your finger, apply a thin bead of grout to the inside edge of the entrance hole. Using the putty knife, spread a smooth, generous layer of grout over the front of the house.

8. Encircle the entrance hole with pebbles, being careful not to obstruct the hole. Then add pebbles randomly, leaving slight spaces between the stones.

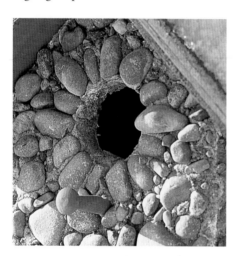

9. Sprinkle tiny pebbles and sand over any spots where grout is still visible. Set the pebbles and sand in the grout with the back of the spoon or your finger. Let dry overnight.

9 *Sprinkle tiny pebbles and sand to cover exposed grout.*

Finishing Touches

10. If the house has a lip or landing around the base, apply a smooth layer of grout and cover with fine sand and gravel.

11. For an optional roof covering, drape pieces of bark over the roof and secure with staples, short nails, or glue as shown.

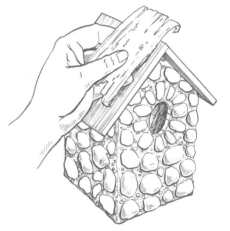

11 *Drape pieces of bark over the roof and secure.*

Variations

- For a different look, cover the roof with small slate shards using the same grout technique.
- Apply the same stone technique to a birdfeeder, but paint, do *not* grout and pebble, the floor of the feeder.
- Make a bolder version of the pebble birdhouse by omitting the tiny pebbles and sand. Start at the top of each side and work your way down in succession using pebbles of similar size and leaving spaces between stones exposed.

toad house

Only four rocks are needed to construct the basic toad starter home. Mansions, of course, require more rocks of larger size. If in doubt about how to build such a structure, ask the closest child or nearest frog.

Choose a shady garden spot, preferably near water and plants. Nestle three rocks into the soil to create the walls, then lay another across the top for the roof. Erect a VACANCY sign to attract homeless toads. Enlist the help of a little landscaper or exterior decorator to make this house a home. A twig chair or arbor can be easily constructed from like-sized twigs. Secure twigs with quick-setting epoxy. Add stepping-stones and small plantings in scale with the house for a designer look.

Linda Lee Purvis

EDDIE FOISY'S ONE-OF-A-KIND PEBBLE CASTLES are magic made real. Individually chosen pebbles and stones are painstakingly mortared into place, and turret-tops are made from copper cones that are shingled with custom-cut shakes. The stone-silled windows often feature stained glass as complementary architectural details. These customized castles take months to complete, and Eddie prefers to personally install them in their new surroundings, so they are positioned just right.

Eddie collects some of his pebbles from a nearby beach, but the bulk of the stones used for facing the walls are purchased. Of every three or four stones he

PEBBLE CASTLES

EDDIE FOISY

handles, only one is considered suitable for obtaining the ideal fit. Each castle is a unique sculpture set into a specific landscape of herbs and foliages selected to enhance the fairytale setting.

Eddie's love of gardening, together with his respect for Nature and her creatures, is inseparable from his passion for creating illusion. Eddie's own Cape Cod garden is a sight to behold, featuring a neighborhood of fairy sanctuaries and isolated fairy doors, strategically placed where bashful sprites can come and go safely, unseen under the cover of lush foliage.

Left: *Each stone for these marvelous miniatures is carefully chosen and painstakingly placed by hand. (Photos by Eddie Foisy)*

9

Children are naturally drawn to the size, shape, and texture of stones. Toddlers who can barely walk will pause, crouch down, pick up a rock, inspect it, and show it off excitedly. Allowing children to explore in this way has tremendous value. Encourage the children in your life to appreciate stones for their uniqueness, while urging them to think creatively about how they might be used.

little pebbles
STONE CRAFTS FOR CHILDREN OF ALL AGES

Describing rocks as little mountains with ancient pasts instills a sense of mystery and wonder. Taking special outings to find and collect rocks becomes an exciting adventure that simply can't be matched when shopping in a craft store. Children's sense of wonder, imagination, and creativity combine to produce cherished treasures that they proudly share. Make stone crafts with them. Share their joy.

stone stamps

RUBBER-STAMPING HAS BECOME enormously popular during the past decade. Crafters use rubber stamps to decorate their own notecards, wrapping paper, fabric — you name it, someone has probably rubber-stamped it. The results are always fun and the technique is suitable for all ages and skill levels.

Stones are a natural choice for stamping. Not only do they serve as nifty, built-in handles for the stamp, but the weight of the stone contributes to the clarity of the stamped image. Choose stones that fit comfortably in little hands and that have at least one flat surface. If stones are gently rounded, select ones with even textures. Avoid stones that are too large or heavy for the artist to handle.

Children will love making their own stamp designs, creating reusable collections of personalized symbols, letters, and images. The stamps themselves are quite eye-catching and are wonderful collectibles. If you've done it before, you know that rubber-stamping is just plain fun. So get started!

MATERIALS

Smooth, flat stones

Paint, acrylic (optional)

Sealer (optional)

Foam sheet (available at craft-supply stores)

EQUIPMENT

Paintbrush (optional)

Pen/pencil

Tracing paper (optional)

Stencil (optional)

Scissors

Rotary cutter (optional)

Glue

Damp cloth

Paper

Decorating the Stone

1. Some children enjoy decorating their stones before they even start making the stamps. Wash the stone well and let it air-dry.
2. Decorate the stone with acrylic paint, and let dry.
3. Protect the design with a good coat of sealer, and let dry thoroughly.

Selecting an Image

Most children have lots of ideas when it comes to selecting an image. But when they're first starting out, some guidance from you might be needed. Here are some things to keep in mind:

• Use simple images; too much detail will be difficult to cut out and glue securely to the rock.

• You don't have to be original. Look for ideas in clip-art books, shape books, and stylized letter books. Look at stencils and traditional rubber stamps.

• If there's a large image that intrigues you, reduce it to just the right size on a photocopier.

• Be creative. Whimsical freehand shapes work well.

• Don't worry about accuracy. Stamps are unique.

• Create designs for backgrounds. For example, use geometric shapes to fill a page, then embellish it with colored pens.

project continues on page 138 ▶

Creating the Stamp

1. Draw or trace the stamp design onto the foam craft sheet. The stamp design should be sized appropriately for the stone.

2. With sharp scissors or rotary cutter, cut out the stamp design from the foam sheet.

3. Glue the shape to the stone, wiping away any excess glue with a damp cloth. Let dry completely.

TIP: Superglue holds foam best, but white glue is more appropriate for young children, particularly if they are doing their own gluing.

Clean stamps with soapy water immediately after use.

Applying the Paint or Ink

Paint or ink can be applied to the stamp in different ways. Using a modest amount of paint or ink will result in sharp images with well-defined edges. Too much paint will pool in the crevices and produce blurry prints. Of course, children will probably enjoy experimenting with their new tools, so let them play to their hearts' content. Following are a few ideas that might help you guide them.

• Use an inkpad. It's the easiest and quickest method to apply color to a stamp. Encourage them to make light, even contact from stamp to pad.

• Dip a paintbrush in paint, and blot the tip on a sheet of paper or a paper towel. Then apply paint directly from the brush to the stamp.

• Lightly paint the middles of paper plates with different colors. While paint is wet, set stamp in the plate and gently rock the stamp back and forth.

Using the Stamp

1. Place a piece of paper or fabric on a flat, smooth surface. A sheet of firm cardboard placed under the paper or fabric will help cushion the print.

2. Lightly brush the stamp with paint or press it on the pad of ink or paint.

3. Carefully press the stamp on the paper or fabric with steady, even pressure. Press rounded stones gently and evenly from side to side.

4. Lift the stamp straight up from the paper or fabric; don't slide the stamp, as this will smear the image.

5. Clean stamps well with soapy water immediately after use. Be careful not to break the glue seal. Use a paintbrush to clean out crevices between the foam pieces. Air dry.

Custom-Made Inkpad

Inkpads are great, but sometimes it's hard to find large ones. Make your own by wrapping a piece of muslin around several layers of felt cut to the size you need. Pin or stitch the back of the muslin to hold it in place. Lay the muslin flat, seam side first, into a plastic container with a tight-fitting lid. Old margarine tubs work well. Drizzle ink or dye into the container until the pad is saturated.

decoupaged rocks

Deciding how to dress up a stone is like trying to choose what to wear for Halloween — the options are almost endless. By first grade, most children already know how to paint, so suggesting that they decorate a rock with paint and something else will be exciting for them. It's a great opportunity for children to experiment with color and texture on a three-dimensional surface, and it's easy!

Encourage children to choose rocks of different sizes and shapes, and remind them that rocks with smooth surfaces are easiest to decorate. Then gather all the materials you'll need: acrylic paints, paintbrushes, magazines (wrapping paper, greeting cards, wallpaper; or pressed leaves and flower petals, found butterfly wings, anything you like), scissors, white glue, and a small container of water. Cover the work surface with several layers of newspaper before you start.

Begin to decoupage with a rock au naturel or have the children paint their rocks. Either way, the rock must be clean and completely dry before you get started.

Have the children cut out their favorite pictures from the magazines. Next, completely coat the back of the picture with glue and apply a thin layer of glue on the rock. Press the picture down lightly with your finger and smooth it to remove wrinkles and excess glue. Then coat the entire surface with diluted white glue (3 parts glue to 1 part water works well) and let dry completely. Continue applying coats of glue until the edges of the pictures are smooth.

Decorating rocks is a great activity for a rainy afternoon and for small groups of children at birthday parties. And the results can be quite beautiful.

If you become an enthusiastic decoupager, try Mod Podge (Norcross, GA: Plaid Enterprises, Inc.). It's easy to apply, and easy to clean up while wet. It glues and seals in one step.

painted rocks

CHILDREN ENJOY LOOKING FOR SHAPES in clouds and can have the same fun looking for hidden images in rocks. Ask them if their rocks resemble anything familiar: a face, an animal, maybe even a cartoon character? Remind them that rocks can stand alone or be used together to make something larger, such as a snowman or a dinosaur. Even the smoothest rock can be dressed up in polka dots or tiger stripes, just for fun.

Newspaper makes a useful covering for a table but sometimes drying paint will stick to it. Instead, set painted rocks on waxed paper to dry. Also, a hair dryer can speed up the drying time if you're working on only a few stones and don't have time to wait for them to air-dry.

MATERIALS

Rocks, preferably smooth

Paint, acrylic

Sealer (optional)

EQUIPMENT

Selection of paintbrushes

Pencil

Paper towels

Container with water

Sponges, stencils, stamps (optional)

1. Wash rocks well, and let air-dry.

2. If using a background color, paint the top and sides of the rock, then let dry. Turn the stone over, then paint the bottom. Let dry.

3. With a pencil, draw lines or shapes that will be painted with a different color. Add one color at a time, being sure to let paint dry completely between colors.

A Word about Paint

Beginners and young children should use nontoxic acrylic paints because they're inexpensive, easy-to-use, and clean up with soap and water. Seasoned painters or older children might enjoy experimenting with enamel, metallic, glow-in-the-dark, or glass paints. For the most part, these require special cleanup and may be toxic if swallowed, so they must be used only with adult supervision but are probably best reserved for more mature children.

pebble candles

A CANDLE'S FLICKERING LIGHT casts lively shadows that children love to watch. But how does the wick get in there? How can a candle burn so long? What's wax made of? Most children haven't the foggiest idea how candles are made, and this project is an excellent opportunity to give them a history lesson and reinforce basic fire safety. The simple poured-wax projects that follow are designed to be fast, fun, and easy and can be made in an afternoon.

MATERIALS

Wax chips or blocks (paraffin, beeswax, other candle wax)

Wick (do *not* use string)

Wick anchor tab or a nail

Small pebbles, approximately ½" (1 cm)

Ice cubes or crushed ice

Clear glass container (for Pebble-Cup Candle)

EQUIPMENT

Metal juice can

Pot or pan

Mold (milk carton, potato-chip can, paper frozen juice can, clear glass container such as votive holder or mason jar)

Scissors

Tape (optional)

Pencil

Oven mitts

Yogurt cup (optional)

Paper towels

Plate

PEBBLE-AND-ICE CANDLE

Aside from the wax and the wick, this candle is made with things you might find in your recycling bin, an excellent example of how to reuse, renew, recycle. This project requires adult supervision.

After successfully making one candle, encourage a child's creativity by experimenting with the procedure. Use different sizes and amounts of ice cubes; substitute crushed ice for ice cubes; use different sizes and colors of pebbles; use different colors of wax; and use a variety of molds with different sizes and shapes. Each change will alter the outcome, with unpredictable results that are sure to brighten your day.

1. Place wax into a clean metal juice can, and set in a pan or pot filled with about 1 to 2 inches (2.5–5 cm) of water. Place pan on burner set to medium-high heat, and melt wax completely. As water evaporates, add more to the pan.

2. Select a candle mold. Milk and juice cartons, potato-chip cans, and paper frozen juice cans are excellent. Different molds allow you to make candles of various sizes and shapes.

3. Cut the wick approximately 2 inches (5 cm) longer than the mold is high. Fasten one end of the wick to an anchor tab, and drop it into the mold. Tie or tape the other end of the wick to a twig or pencil that straddles the top of the mold. *Note:* Ideally the wick will be placed in the center of the mold and there will be no slack.

4. Add enough pebbles to the mold to cover the wick anchor and mold bottom.

project continues on page 144 ▶

5. Add a few ice cubes to the mold, then more pebbles, alternating until you come to the desired height or within half an inch (1.3 cm) of the top of the mold.

6. With oven mitts, carefully grasp the container of wax and remove from pot. Scoop melted wax into a small yogurt cup and then pour into the candle mold. Fill the mold until pebbles and ice are covered, but leave at least ½-inch (1.3 cm) of space from the top of the mold. Place the mold in the refrigerator and let chill for 15 minutes. If it's cold where you are, you can also place the container outside to chill.

7. Return the wax container to the pan of water, and add more wax if necessary. Warm the pan at medium-high heat until the wax is completely melted.

8. After 15 minutes have passed, check to see if a well has formed at the top of the candle. If so, use oven mitts to grasp container of wax and pour more wax to fill well and bring to desired height. Let mold chill for about an hour.

9. Remove twig or pencil from the wick. Trim wick to about ¼ inch (0.6 cm).

10. Remove candle from the mold by cutting the topmost edge and gently peeling downward. This is best done over a sink or bowl, as the water from the melted ice cubes will spill out.

11. Place a few paper towels on a plate, and let candle air dry. *Note:* Part of the charm of this candle comes from the air pockets formed by the ice cubes. It's a fragile candle, however, so handle it with care.

PEBBLE-CUP CANDLE

This fast-and-easy project was inspired by candles infused with herbs and flower petals. Instead of using a disposable mold, this time you'll use a clear glass container, such as a votive holder or Mason jar, to contain the candle. The color and texture of the pebbles peek through the wax and glass.

1. Choose a clear glass container.

2. Follow steps 1–3 of the Pebble-and-Ice Candle instructions on page 143 to melt the wax and prepare the wick.

3. Fill the glass container loosely, to the desired candle height, with pebbles. Carefully pour in melted wax to cover them. Let candle set for 15 minutes, then check to see if a well has formed. Add more wax if necessary. Let candle harden for about an hour.

4. Trim wick to about ¼ inch (0.6 cm).

Fire Safety

- Fire is dangerous.
- *Never* play with matches or lighters.
- *Never* leave a lit candle unattended.

PEBBLE MOSAIC VOTIVE

This is a fun project for children who enjoy getting their hands dirty.

MATERIALS

Glass container
Mortar patch compound
Small pebbles
Votive candle

EQUIPMENT

Putty knife or spreader
Container of water

1. Scoop a generous amount of mortar patch onto the putty knife.

2. Apply mortar to the exterior of the glass container, starting at the rim and working down. Don't cover the base with mortar. Set putty knife in container of water for easy cleanup.

3. Decorate mortar with pebbles, pressing pebbles in just enough to secure them. Let dry.

4. Place a standard votive candle into the container.

story stones

The imagination is a powerful thing. Kids tap into it instinctively. As adults, we sometimes need a bit of prodding to think imaginatively. Story stones are a clever way to combine a creative hand and a fertile imagination.

At your next campfire gathering or some quiet evening at home, have everyone draw imaginary symbols, letters, figures, or markings onto individual stones using paint, gel pens, markers, or anything that can write on stone. When the stones dry, collect them in a pouch or hat, and have each participant randomly select a stone. Take turns telling stories that explain the historical significance or origin of the image on the stone — the more fantastic, the better. You'll be surprised at what you learn.

At every opportunity, invite the children in your life to teach you. Surrender your logical mind to their imagination, and enjoy. Story stones are food for the imagination.

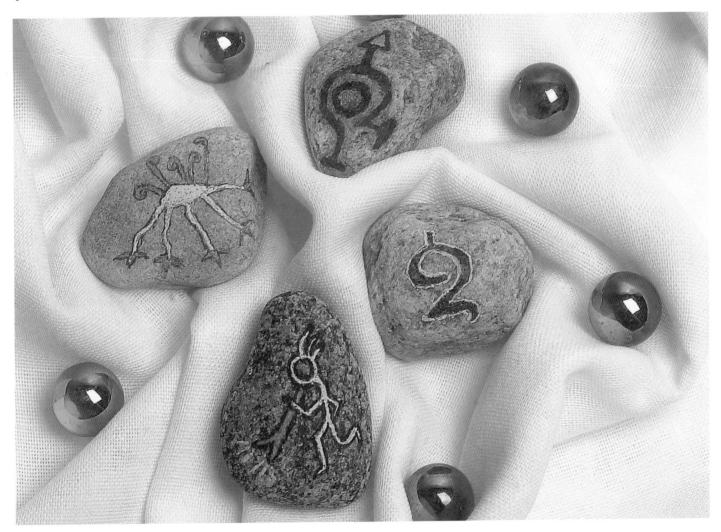

A RESIDENT OF GREENFIELD, MASSACHUSETTS, Matthew Leighton is not a trained artist, that is to say, not trained beyond age ten when he finished elementary school. In 1990, shortly after turning fifty, he made his first assemblage — a six-foot fish composed of squashed beer cans — to commemorate the twentieth anniversary of Earth Day. Since then he has made more than three hundred pieces using an uninhibited inventory of collected, found, and donated odds and ends.

It wasn't until he spent some time visiting Cape Cod nine years later that he found beach stones to be an irresistible depository of assemblagists' gold. This realization motivated him to help the stones transcend their lives as humble beach fare, using them to create animated characters that resemble light-hearted snapshot moments from TV sitcoms. He gives life to his pictures by carefully considering, in precise, puzzlelike piles, the pebbles to be organized. Plywood backgrounds are

STONE ASSEMBLAGES
MATTHEW LEIGHTON

painted in vivid colors that scream at viewers from behind what might otherwise be understated compositions of natural stones. Pebbles and stones are glued in place for a result like no other.

Photos by Lewis Baker

recommended reading

Adkins, Dorcas. *Simple Fountains.* Pownal, VT: Storey, 1999.

Andrews, Ted. *Animal Speak: The Spiritual & Magical Powers of Creatures Great & Small.* St. Paul, MN: Llewellyn, 1993.

Black, Penny. *The Book of Potpourri: Fragrant Flower Mixes for Scenting and Decorating the Home.* New York: Simon & Schuster, 1989.

Codina, Carles. *The Complete Book of Jewelry Making.* Asheville, NC: Lark, 2000.

Davies, Patricia. *Aromatherapy — An A to Z Guide.* Essex, UK: C. W. Daniels Company, 1999.

Hallendy, Norman. *Inuksuit: Silent Messengers of the Arctic.* Seattle: University of Washington Press, 2000.

Hillier, Malcolm. *The Book of Fresh Flowers.* New York: Simon & Schuster, 1988.

Mack, Daniel. *Making Rustic Furniture.* Asheville, NC: Lark, 1992.

Marshall, Marlene Hurley. *Making Bits and Pieces Mosaics.* Pownal, VT: Storey, 1998.

McGrath, Jinks. *The Encyclopedia of Jewelry-Making Techniques.* Philadelphia: Running Press, 1995.

Meadows, Kenneth. *Rune Power.* Boston: Element Books, 1996.

Mella, Dorothee. *Stone Power.* New York: Warner, 1994.

Nielson, Greg, and Joseph Polansky. *Pendulum Power.* New York: HarperCollins, 1987.

Ohrbach, Barbara Milo. *The Scented Room.* New York: Clarkson N. Potter, 1986.

Olsen, Dale. *Knowing Your Intuitive Mind.* Eugene, OR: Crystalline Publications, 1999.

Pennick, Nigel. *The Complete Illustrated Guide to Runes.* London: Thorsons, 1999.

Phillips, Sue. *Healing Stones.* Berks, UK: Capall Bann, 1998.

Reed, David. *The Art and Craft of Stonescaping.* Asheville, NC: Lark, 1998.

Wallace, Mary. *The Inuksuk Book.* Eugene, OR: Crystalline Publications, 1999.

Worwood, Valerie Ann. *The Fragrant Pharmacy.* New York: Bantam Books, 1990.

resource guide

Advantage
4270 Aloma Avenue — 124 Suite 33B
Winter Park, FL 32792
Phone: 407-678-1177 Fax: 407-678-7414
Manufacturer of diamond and carbide cutting tools

Artistic Wire
1210 Harrison Avenue
La Grange Park, IL 60526
Phone: 630-530-7567 Fax: 630-530-7536
Large variety of permanently colored copper wire

Bourget Jewelry
1636 11th Street
Santa Monica, CA 90404
Phone: 800-828-3024
Web: www.bourgetbros.com
Jewelry and craft supplies; adhesives, cords, chains, tools

Ceramics and Creative Crafts
12900 Regional Road No. 39
Zephyr, ON L0E 1T0
CANADA
Phone: 905-473-2024
Web: www.ceramic.on.ca
Unpainted bisque, paints, rusting medium

Curry's Art Store, Ltd.
2345 Stanfield Road, Unit 3
Mississauga, ON L4Y 3Y3
CANADA
Phone: 416-798-7983 Fax: 905-272-0778
Web: www.currys.com
Complete line of artists' supplies

Dad's Rock Shop
P.O. Box 10649
Ft. Mohave, AR 86427
Phone: 800-844-3237
Web: www.dadsrockshop.com
Lapidary equipment; tools, tumblers, jewelry findings

D. S. Martin Mechanical
176 Bullock Drive, Unit #12
Markham, ON L3P 7N1
CANADA
Fax: 905-471-4266
Custom sheet metal fabricators

Fountain Mountain
439 Wellington
Santa Maria, CA 93455
Phone: 805-934-4565 Fax: 800-853-2353
Web: www.fountainmountain.com
Fountain-making supplies, table fountain pumps

Lamp Specialties
P.O. Box 240
Westville, NJ 08093-0240
Phone: 856-931-1253
Web: www.lamp-specialties.com
Lamp accessories, lamp bottle kits

Mannion's Indoor Fountain and Book Supply
P.O. Box 362864
San Diego, CA 92163
Phone: 800-828-5967 Fax: 619-280-7711
Web: www.buildfountains.com
Fountain-making supplies, pumps, stones

Mainly Shades
100 Gray Road
Falmouth, ME 04105
Phone: 207-797-7568
Lamp supplies, shade frames, bottle kits

Marble Plus, Inc.
66 Drumlin Circle
Concord, ON L4K 3K9
CANADA
Phone: 905-669-9575 Fax: 905-669-9592
Customized stone countertops; stone drilling; can order diamond drill bits

Nature's Expression
#123–11071 Bridgeport Road
Richmond, BC V6X 1T3
Phone: 604-278-6403
Natural rock giftware, rock tumblers

Odyssey Books and Resource Centre
109 Old Kingston Road, Unit #15
Ajax, ON L1T 3A6
CANADA
Phone: 905-426-4823
Web: www.odysseybooks.on.ca
Books, runes, pendulums, stones, jewelry

Spirit West Enterprises
P.O. Box 42014
Victoria, BC V8R 6T4
CANADA
Phone: 250-544-2093 Fax: 250-544-2039
Animal totem stones, petroglyph stones, jewelry

Stones Studio
P.O. Box 878
Stowe, VT 05672
Phone: 802-888-3909 Fax: 802-888-4136
Web: www.stones-studio.com
Fountains, and art from natural stone

The Wax House
236 Arch Avenue
Waynesboro, VA 22980
Phone: 888-WAX-9711 (888-929-9711)
Web: www.waxhouse.com
Candlemaking supplies

Wellington Way Rental
6080 Highway #7
Markham, ON L3P 3B1
CANADA
Rental equipment; tile-cutting saws

index

contributing artists

Katherine Ahern
Birch and Willow
30 Cottage Street
Wellesley, MA 02482
Phone: 617-423-3437
E-mail: birchandwillow
  @att.net
Handmade lamps from wood, vine, and stone; see page 81

Dan Ansems
Creations by Dingo
Belmont, ON N0L 1B0
CANADA
Phone: 519-269-9670
Forging and ironwork with stone; see pages 20, 127

**ArtStone by
Gabriel Cortez**
Natural Stone Mosaics
231 O'Donoghue Ave.
Oakville, ON LGH 3W5
CANADA
Phone: 905-849-1995
Web: www.pathcom.com/~artstone/
Murals, tables, floors, garden ornaments; see pages 34–35

Lori-Anne Crittenden
1188 Cragg Road
Greenbank, ON L0C 1B0
CANADA
Decorative painting on stone; work not pictured.

Eddie Foisy
P.O. Box 96
Harwichport, MA 02646
Web: www.
  uncleeddiesworld.com
Pebble castles; see pages 132–33

Laurie Heath
Ladybird Designs
1244A Bayview Street
Pickering, ON L1W 1E6
CANADA
E-mail: laurieladybird@sympatico.ca
Jewelry design; see pages 120–21

Bill Kunnas
12125 Highway #48
Stouffville, ON L4A 7X5
CANADA
Custom twig furniture and accessories; see page 12

Mark Richardson
Marked in Stone
Newmarket, ON
CANADA
Phone: 905-868-8030
Sandblasting and custom stone engraving; see pages 52, 70, 102–3

Matthew Leighton
28 Lillian Street
Greenfield, MA 01301
Assemblagist; see pages 146–47

Glen Simmons
Transformations
Phone: 905-687-0440 or 416-727-7242
Natural paper lampshades; work not pictured

Jean-Jacques Ferron
Modern Stone Age
54 Greene Street
New York, NY 10013
Phone: 212-219-0383
Web: www.modern-stone.com
Conceptual stone art; see pages 54–55

Note: Some contact information has been omitted at the request of the artist.